Praise for David A. Giersdorf and *Hard Ships*

"Thank you for this voyage plan, David. Your prescience and clear-eyed vision have confidently charted the course for many of us for years in this industry, and the timing of your book couldn't be better. Like spotting the safe harbor entrance after a perilous passage . . ."

—Michael Bennett
Captain, Consultant, Author

"Any tough situation, hard to solve problem, fear for my business . . . gets the same response. Call David Giersdorf. Over my lifetime he has shaped my leadership abilities to get out of challenging situations. Through *Hard Ships*, David distills his forty years of successfully dealing with jaw-dropping challenges into several important concepts that can help any leader, current or future, keep their cool when it is needed the most. I highly recommend this insightful book."

—Bill Fritsch
Former CEO, Digital Kitchen, 3-Time Emmy Award Winning Communications Agency

"As a journalist covering the cruise industry, I've begun following David when he was at Windstar and Holland America but really got a chance to see him work when he was launching Ambassadors. What struck me then was his enthusiasm, unabashed fascination with anything cruise-related, and ability to think creatively."

—Carolyn Spencer Brown
Former Editor-in-Chief, Cruise Critic, a TripAdvisor Company

"David simplifies the distinction between chaos and clarity. We all are living through a time of disturbance. Read this for a guide to clarity for you and those you care for. When the world makes it very hard to see where to steer, David has practical lessons on how to make your way and succeed on the other side of the storms."

—Mark Kammerer
President, Kammerer Group

"David is a travel industry veteran who has worked with some of the biggest brands in the space, including Holland America Line, Windstar, and more. He's a person that understands the brands he represents, but more importantly, how to effectively market those brands in today's world. He's out in front of current trends that go beyond travel and can add value to any organization."

—Mark Murphy
Serial Entrepreneur

"David is one of the best individuals to provide perspectives in navigating one's career and life. He, quite literally, has seen hard times across his business life as well as personal and brings an authentic expertise, candor, and personal perspectives that help anyone. From his time in politics and criss-crossing the State of Washington to understand and immerse himself in the lives of those across the State; to the ups and downs of the cruise & travel industry impacted by new innovations, changing demographics, environmental aspects and now COVID-19; to deeply personal family and life challenges that would stop anyone . . . David brings perspectives and expertise with deep empathy and understanding that helps provide a navigation path for us all . . . particularly amidst the challenging and uncertain times in which we all find ourselves."

—Matt Abrams
Investor, Advisor, Board Member, Innovator, Coach

"David has an unopened gift that he has presented to all those in the travel industry who are willing to unwrap this present. He combines a lifetime of both cruise industry and cruise passenger knowledge, with a broad range of experiences across many cruise operators, to unlock the key to navigating uncertain and highly competitive waters. Read and listen to him speak and you will reap the rewards. This book should be on the desk of any cruise industry executive."

—Bill Spaeth
Cruise Ship Marketing Executive with 25+ years of experience

"David is well known as one of the pioneers in the cruise industry, and specifically in the pacific northwest. I relied on his advice and counsel extensively while he was Executive Vice President of Holland America Line and I was President of the International Council of Cruise Lines. He is a true professional."

—Michael Crye
Principal at independent public and regulatory affairs consultancy focused on maritime industry

"I have known and worked with David for over thirty years, starting with a small Seattle based tour company in the 1970s where I worked with David running the Alaska operations. David is one of the most creative marketing minds I know. Over the years, has pursued his career with a passion and love of life and learning. David has both strong operational and creative experience, and a talent to quickly evaluate new opportunities with a good balance of the possibilities and practicalities."

—Tad Lewis
Principal, GuidePoint Law

"David Giersdorf is a cruise industry veteran and a pioneer. He is well-known throughout the industry for his strong leadership, unquestionable devotion, entrepreneurial spirit, award-winning marketing, and supreme desire to provide every guest who steps aboard every ship with a magical cruise experience."

—**Ron Elgin**
Board of Directors Member

"I first worked together with David when he was appointed as Vice President, Sales and Marketing for Windstar Cruises, a subsidiary of Holland America Line, back in the early 90s. David was the main reason that made Windstar one of the elite cruise lines with adequate profit margin every year.

"I worked together with David for the second time when he came back to Holland America Line as the Senior Vice President, Sales & Marketing in the early 2000s. During his tenure, Holland America Line doubled up its capacity to become not only one of the largest passenger cruise lines, but also the most profitable line in the world.

"David is very intelligent, hard-working, and always has a clear vision of what he would want to accomplish with a great character of integrity. He has always led his teams by example, and is one of the most creative business leaders as I know of."

—**James Yang**
Former Partner

"David has an astute business mind and the instincts of a true entrepreneur. He builds strong teams and strong businesses. I admire his character, determination, and myriad professional skills. His performance elevates the performance of those around him. He inspires confidence and produces results."

—**Tim Pavish**
Executive Director, Washington State University Alumni Association

"I worked with David for a number of years and we communicated during that period about a wide variety of issues affecting our business relationship, including sales, marketing, contracts, and the competitive environment. He demonstrated particular competence in high-level business strategy and marketing."

—Emerson Kirksey Hankamer
Chief Executive Officer, Vacations To Go

HARD SHIPS

Bob -
It is my good
fortune and priveledge
to count you as a friend.
I look forward to future
opportunities to spend time
together. Warmly,

Owl Gut

Do the opposite of nothing. Be the opposite of helpless.

HARD SHIPS

NAVIGATING YOUR COMPANY, CAREER, AND LIFE THROUGH THE FOG OF DISRUPTION

David A. Giersdorf

Bend, OR

Hard Ships copyright © 2021 by David A. Giersdorf

Giersdorf Group LLC

Suite 500, 10400 NE 4th Street

Bellevue, WA 98004

Publisher's Cataloging-In-Publication Data

   Names: Giersdorf, David A., author.

   Title: Hard ships : navigating your company, career, and life through the
      fog of disruption / David A. Giersdorf.

   Description: Bend, Oregon : Giersdorf Group LLC, [2021] | Includes
      bibliographical references.

   Identifiers: ISBN 9781736374108 (softcover paperback) | ISBN 9781736374115
      (jacketed case laminate hardcover) | ISBN 9781736374122 (Kindle ebook)

   Subjects: LCSH: Change (Psychology) | Life change events--Psychological
      aspects. | Crisis management. | Giersdorf, David A.--Career in tourism.
      | Cruise lines--Economic aspects.

   Classification: LCC BF637.C4 G54 2021 (print) | LCC BF637.C4 (ebook) | DDC
      158.1--dc23

Special discounts for bulk sales are available.
Please email Contact@DavidGiersdorf.com.

To my Father, Robert Giersdorf, who was a Master of Disruption—creating it and responding to it—throughout his businesses, his career, and his personal life. In fact, his last words to me in the hospital ICU a few days before his passing were, "I want a fighting chance." That, in a few words, sums up the spirit of my Father. I miss his bigger-than-life energy, powerfully positive outlook, and fearlessness to this day.

This one's for you, Dad.

5 Ways to Get David's Help Directly

Want free updates from the author? Join David A. Giersdorf's email list for up-to-date, need-to-know cruise, travel, and tourism industry news. You'll also be notified about new products such as the upcoming *Hard Ships* masterclass. Simply subscribe at www.DavidGiersdorf.com.

Ready to align your team with a proven process to outlast disruption? Buy *Hard Ships* for your organization, leadership team, C-suite, board, team, or family. Email Contact@DavidGiersdorf.com for more information.

Need a guest speaker to inspire your team? Request David A. Giersdorf to speak at your event, deliver a workshop, or address your team remotely. Email Contact@DavidGiersdorf.com for more info.

Want expert advice? Get David A. Giersdorf's advisory services for your C-suite or board. Expertise includes growth, performance, product development, acquisitions, marketing, sales, distribution, and emerging technologies.

David is also available to implement his recommendations with his hand-picked team to create your bespoke solution. Email Contact@DavidGiersdorf.com for more.

Need more revenue? Access the Global Voyages Group proprietary marketing database for cruise, travel, and tourism marketers. Contact David@GlobalVoyagesGroup.com.

Contents

Foreword

By Jack Anderson

There are leaders who lead from the front and leaders who lead from behind. In rare cases, there are leaders who are willing to roll up their sleeves and jump into the middle while leading from both the front and behind. That's David Giersdorf. I've always been taken with David's ability to both honor the board room and captivate a crew on a ship while crafting all the critical consumer touch points that deliver a world-class customer experience. It all matters to David.

I've been in the brand consulting design world for forty-six years. I co-founded a company called Hornall Anderson Design Works thirty-eight years ago. Today, I'm Executive Chairman of Sid Lee USA, one of the curated companies in the KYU Collective. Over that period of time, I've had the privilege to consult in all types of industries alongside many types of leaders. Clients have ranged from global coffee companies to airlines to cruise companies to technology companies to lifestyle companies, to sports franchises to countless consumer brands. Size of company has ranged from startups to Fortune 100 and pretty much everything in between. Engagements have ranged from four months to thirty-three years. Suffice it to say, I've seen it all—leadership styles, etc.—and I can say that David is truly among the best. I'm thrilled that he's written a book to share his knowledge with the world.

I know David as a devoted husband, a passionate father, a competitive athlete, and a wise, compelling businessman. *Everything* he takes on, he approaches with 100 percent commitment and a team mindset. His drive, compassion, and commitment to lead by example while bringing others on the journey has fostered best-in-class, category-breaking solutions and outcomes.

I first met David when we were selected as part of a larger team to reposition Windstar Sail Cruises, a fledgling new cruise brand that was struggling to find a financially viable combination of product concept, destinations, itineraries, and market position. David quarterbacked the entire effort that led to the crafting of Windstar Cruises as one of the most iconic and successful boutique cruise brands in the industry. His strategy was encapsulated by the positioning, "180 Degrees From Ordinary." The brilliance of that line gave the full team the permission, the responsibility, if you will, to deliver unique, ownable solutions in everything we created. At a time when predictable pictures of staterooms and food buffets crowded the market, Windstar's repositioning, from advertising to brochures to the shipboard experience, was unique and world-class by every definition. David would later create "Signature Of Excellence" for Holland America. In all cases, David's strategic vision and leadership have achieved breakthrough results.

David's approach to life is to push on the edges, all the edges. He looks for the truth, the opportunity, and the critical sauce that will make the difference. He views challenges as opportunities. His unusual combination of beginner's mindset and seasoned practitioner leads to unique breakthrough outcomes.

I've been fortunate to have worked with countless clients and consultants over the past forty-six years. Many lean on what they did the last time. While there's nothing wrong with drawing from your collective experience, each assignment or opportunity deserves a crisp, fresh look at the problem to be solved, the competition, the obstacles, and most importantly, *the opportunity*. In my experience, few check all the boxes like David. I consider him a mentor, an explorer, an alchemist, and a close friend.

—**Jack Anderson**
Executive Chairman, Sid Lee USA

Preface

"The Ship of My Soul" Poem

In November 2003, I wrote the following journal entry:

Today, while running on a fabulously sunny, crisp fall afternoon, I had the thought that this year has been my perfect storm—a convergence of elements to test the extremes of my character and soul. What a very tough and very expansive year it has been. While running, I composed the following poem:

The Ship of My Soul

A perfect storm
Not expected
Crashes down
Wave after wave
Of loss and grief
Pounding me with despair

Save the ship! I think
Bail, Steer, Repair
Repeat

Parents struggled one by one
Drew last breaths as I stood near
My illusion of control
Gone with them

Impermanence made clear
Bolts of enlightenment
From the sky
My shield of denial
Swept away

A son leaves home
On his life's journey
I learn to let him go

The compass of my life
Begins to spin
I watch with fascination

The ship of my soul
Rides through the storm
Cresting each brutal wave

The storm takes on a beauty of its own
Precious lessons in its depths
My ship becomes the sea
I steer a new course
To horizons once beyond my imagining

Dear reader, I do understand the impact of loss, setbacks, and change in one's business, career, and life. It can be most difficult, and at times, overwhelming. I also know the way through to a successful outcome, to a continuation of the journey to new horizons. Let's make a voyage of discovery together and steer a new course in the pages that follow.

CHAPTER 1

Into the Fog

A ship in harbor is safe, but that is not what ships are built for.
—John A. Shedd

The cruise industry sails into its busiest booking season every January and February, appropriately known as "wave season." In the cold, dark Northern Hemisphere, people with the means to vacation start planning their next one. They can't wait to enjoy the world's most memorable sites from the luxurious comfort of a cruise ship. Whether the ship is headed for exotic Pacific islands, central European waterways, the clear blue Caribbean, or Alaska's awesome scenery, the simple act of clicking "book now" on a cruise package brings a rush of excitement. New experiences are on the way.

In 2019, the world traveled like never before. That meant the highest revenue year on record for the cruise industry. As expected, 2020 also started strong. January and February bookings put cruise lines worldwide on track for an even bigger and better year. As a senior executive and adviser to the cruise industry, I had continuous discussions with cruise-line clients looking for ways to optimize this incredible growth. Some wanted to expand even further. How do we break out from competitors, engage even more customers, and leverage new technologies to offer the cruise experience of the future today? With the tide of demand only rising, cruise and travel executives focused on positioning their companies to meet it.

But growth management wasn't the only topic that came up in our conversations. In early January, all my client discussions ended the same way. After asking my advice on a new ship build to increase cruise capacity or a creative rebrand to appeal to a different customer segment, these clients would ask me, "So, David . . . what do you think about this new virus?"

I'll be honest. I thought the same as they did—"Heads up!" The news of a respiratory infection afflicting many thousands in mainland China circulated through our industry faster than others. Any virus is bad news for travel in general and for cruises specifically. Viruses of all types are already a top health and safety challenge on ships. You can imagine why. Viruses are extremely contagious. A respiratory virus is potentially deadly for the most vulnerable travelers, those who are older or dealing with medical challenges. People over the age of sixty are a large proportion of cruise-line guests since they're more likely to have the discretionary budget and the time to take cruises. Cruise ships have well-equipped medical facilities and professionals, but they're not hospitals. Anyone with preexisting health conditions who develops severe respiratory symptoms may require intensive and extended medical care.

Sometimes quarantines can happen, though rarely, if there's a bad viral outbreak aboard a cruise ship. Health authorities may stop a cruise in progress and cancel future cruises until all guests and crew members on that ship have tested negative (or been treated if they were sick). Then that ship has to be sanitized top to bottom and inspected to prevent any recurrence. Even a common norovirus can disrupt the cruise industry.

But in early January 2020, we didn't know how very infectious and dangerous the so-called novel coronavirus was. Sure, it was a concern, but even the experts suggested it was most likely manageable in view of previous outbreaks like SARS-1 and H1N1. Very serious, but nothing our industry hadn't dealt with before. Still, we didn't know how it was contracted or how soon symptoms could appear after infection. By month's end, the public learned that this was no regular flu. Cell phone videos from China went viral on social media, showing a military-style response. Small armies of hazmat-suited workers dragged the sick away from their families into quarantine at gunpoint. When hospitals ran out of room, the police walled up entire apartment buildings, sealing the infected inside. It was like something from a horror movie. Waves of fear reached the West before the virus itself docked here.

China's extreme containment tactics implied that the coronavirus was uniquely contagious—and lethal. It felt like we truly were about to witness a sequel to severe acute respiratory syndrome (SARS), which affected the industry from 2002 to 2003. A respiratory virus with flu- and pneumonia-like symptoms (and also first identified in China) spread to more than two dozen countries in Asia, Europe, and the Americas. The epidemic sank the Asia-Pacific cruise industry until July 2003, when the outbreak was officially contained. At the time, I was a senior executive with Holland America Line. We dropped Shanghai and Hong Kong from our itineraries to avoid visiting areas considered high risk for SARS and revised cruises to call instead at other ports like Okinawa, Japan, and Vladivostok, Russia. We also followed expanded safety pro- tocols, including prohibiting guests from boarding if they had been to Hong Kong, Singapore, or China in the past ten days. And anyone who had been in Toronto during the previous ten days had to answer specific health-screening questions.

Fast forward to early 2020 and the new virus. This was a human biosecurity emergency. One thing was certain: cruising was in for a bumpy ride. We just didn't know how bumpy or for how long. Grow- ing concern among cruise executives, investors, and travelers arrived in my inbox and voice mail daily. *Is this new virus going to show up on a ship? What if our ship is going into a port where the virus is present and guests bring it back on board?* Many also wondered about their operational response and the revenue impact. *Do we take action now with increased safety measures and cancellations? Or wait and see what develops? Pull back on marketing because people aren't booking? Should we lower prices to respond to the change in consumer behavior?*

Our $45 billion industry was already hypersensitive to any guests or crew members with any sickness. In the first days of 2020, all we could do was monitor the situation. All crew members stepped up on symptom observation. Cold symptoms, nausea, and low-grade fevers were noted and carefully monitored. It was clear that cruise operators could not be too careful in the face of this emerging illness.

Cruise lines, including my clients, implemented additional guest protection such as continuously wiping down elevator buttons, railings, and other surfaces with disinfectants. The movement of crew between ships was restricted to avoid a worst-case scenario, multi-ship viral spread. Guest dining procedures were changed—instead of self-serve buffets where everybody touched the same serving utensils, servers behind the counter placed food on all the plates.

In mid-January, the industry's hopes remained high that it would manage this outbreak. With extra safety measures, we believed the cruise industry's projected growth would continue, making 2020 even more profitable than cruising's best year ever.

Then it happened. The first case of novel coronavirus on a cruise ship. On January 20, an eighty-year-old passenger from Hong Kong stepped aboard the *Diamond Princess*, a grand cruise ship owned and operated by Princess Cruises. This guest, who tested positive for the novel coronavirus after sailing one segment of the itinerary, embarking in Yokohama and disembarking five days later in Hong Kong, unknowingly transmitted the virus to other passengers. On February 4, ten other passengers were diagnosed with this new respiratory infection called SARS-CoV-2 or COVID-19 (COVID). That very day, the ship was quarantined in Japan's port of Yokohama. Since everyone was confined on the ship together, more people became sick. Over the ensuing weeks, the infection spread to 712 out of 3,711 passengers and crew, killing 14.

During the initial stages of the COVID-19 pandemic, the *Diamond Princess* was the setting of the largest outbreak outside mainland China. Healthy guests trapped onboard took to social media to share, vlog, and tweet their harrowing experience, seemingly surrounded by the sick and dying. Intense coverage by mainstream news networks and subsequent public concern led all cruise lines to publish travel advisories on their websites. Cruise operators made contingency plans to alter or cancel all Asia-Pacific cruises through spring. Despite the deep concern and publicity, the coronavirus outbreak seemed like a localized event. There were no global showstoppers yet. Perhaps there was still a chance to prevent the spread outside Asia and SARS part two.

As late as February 17, I had back-and-forths with clients about marketing. One asked me about sending emails to past guests promoting a new itinerary that steered clear of Asia. Another asked my advice regarding going forward with a new cruise announcement featuring Antarctica. I suggested they hold off to see how the situation expanded globally. In every business, there are risks. That's a given. The trouble was the cruise industry didn't know if they were facing a short-term localized situation or a long-term global disruption during which *all* cruises would be affected.

A few days later, on February 21, we saw a big red flag. The Centers for Disease Control and Prevention (CDC) officially recommended avoiding travel on cruise ships in Southeast Asia. Luckily, cruise companies were already implementing intense health and safety procedures and making future contingency plans. But things were about to go from bad to worse.

In mid-March, the *Ruby Princess* cruise ship docked in Sydney, Australia. Local health authorities failed to prevent dozens of passengers with COVID-19 symptoms from going to shore. That same week, nineteen crew members and two passengers on the *Grand Princess* off the coast of San Francisco showed COVID symptoms—nausea, body aches, sore throat, dry cough. They tested positive. California state and national health authorities refused to make the same mistake that was made with the *Diamond Princess*. All passengers and crew members were quarantined on board.

Eventually, all three ships—*Diamond*, *Ruby*, and *Grand*—docked, and all guests were quarantined either at home or in medical facilities if required. But the damage was done. For the cruise industry, there was no going back to normal. Passengers who'd booked cruises throughout

2020 suddenly didn't want to take the risk. Even if you don't fall ill, nobody wants to be stranded far away from home, family, and sufficient medical care for weeks because someone onboard tested positive for the virus.

Then it got worse. On March 8, the CDC broadened their travel advisory, recommending that people with underlying health conditions and anyone sixty-five or older stay off cruise ships. A tidal wave of cancellations hit cruise companies in the days that followed—even for cruises with itineraries as far away from China as Antarctica and Greenland. Most companies in the cruise industry have a policy of giving a partial refund for cancellations or offering a credit for a future cruise. The industry saw more cancellations in the two weeks following that CDC recommendation than during the entirety of SARS-1. Our entire industry had to revisit refund policies, taking care to be fair to customers without depleting all available cash, similar to a run on the banks during a financial crisis.

Then it got even worse. On March 13, the Cruise Lines International Association called for a voluntary thirty-day suspension of all cruise operations in the United States. Then the CDC issued a Level 3 travel warning on March 17, recommending the suspension of all cruise travel. Little did we know that date would be forever marked as the day the seas went quiet. That initial order came with a thirty-day limit. Cruises already underway were allowed to end, but new ones couldn't start.

Still, we all thought it would sort itself out. We could bounce back. Only thirty days, right? But how in the world do you bring a multibillion-dollar industry to a halt, only to receive the all clear one month later? You don't. Most companies canceled cruises through the end of April. As time went on, it was all we could do to hang on, grasping for any new or hopeful information. But in early April, the CDC issued the no-sail order, extending the cruise pause.

That's when we knew COVID-19 was here to stay. The SARS-1 scare began to pale by comparison. Publicly traded cruise lines sought liquidity from every source imaginable, issuing new stock and borrowing billions of dollars at unattractive interest rates to ensure they would be able to refund customers and maintain their fleets and companies during a protracted and unprecedented nonoperating period. They also took steps to defer costs of every type and searched for new ways to generate revenue, including selling ships at steeply discounted prices. Meanwhile, the industry with a $45 billion annual revenue plummeted to an annualized loss of $25 billion and a cumulative decline in stock market value among the big three of $65 billion.

There were many in the cruise and leisure travel industry who remained optimistic. In private conversations, executives, founders, and investors told me the market would return to pre-pandemic metrics within one or two years at the most. Thus, they focused on preserving and replicating the business models and practices of the past while waiting and hoping for improvement that would be slow to come.

I had a different vision of the future. In my view, consumers were more informed and cautious than at any time in the past, especially those who traditionally purchased cruise and travel experiences. Competition for their trust, discretionary time, and dollars would be much more intense across all product and service categories. The cost of going to market would effectively increase.

Nine months into the crisis, most business leaders collectively realized there was no going back. Even the dreamers dropped their faith in a return to normal when management consulting firm McKinsey & Company offered color commentary together with predictions, which have already begun coming to pass:

> Barring any unexpected catastrophes, individuals, businesses, and society can start to look forward to shaping their futures rather than just grinding through the present. The next normal is going to be different. It will not mean going back to the conditions that prevailed in 2019. Indeed, just as the terms "prewar" and "postwar" are commonly used to describe the 20th century, generations to come will likely discuss the pre–COVID-19 and post–COVID-19 eras.[1]

---

1 "The Next Normal Arrives: Trends That Will Define 2021—and Beyond," McKinsey & Company, January 4, 2021, www.mckinsey.com/featured-insights/leadership/the-next-normal-arrives-trends-that-will-define-2021-and-beyond#.

How does an industry built on travel survive when there isn't any for months? Every meeting, every call, and every email conversation with my clients was about the damn virus. We became sponges for new information and insight, internal and external. At the same time, we had to make decisions with imperfect information. Nobody had the first clue when the pandemic would end. In such circumstances, your guiding light is always the culture of your company. You've made a promise to your guests and other key stakeholders about the kind of company you are and must perform in accordance with those values. The whole industry was trying to run their businesses and had nothing but questions.

We'd found ourselves lost at sea in a thick fog of disruption. Cruise bans later extended into summer and then fall, and we had to face a terrible truth: at best, the cruise industry was months away from rebooting and years away from recovery. We would be in the fog for a while.

But, as the saying goes, the only way out is through.

• • • •

Have you ever gotten lost in fog? Literal fog? I've been stuck in thick fog twice in my life. Both times were terrifying. The first time was on a boat. Navigating through foggy, narrow passageways, even with radar, you feel totally isolated. Nothing is certain except the impending doom and your heart beating out of your chest. The second time was piloting a helicopter. Fog rolled in suddenly, and clear skies gave way to clear and present danger I couldn't see. I felt ill-equipped and at-risk both times.

Being stuck in the fog is overwhelming and frustrating because you seem blocked on all sides and can't see what's headed right toward you. The onslaught of COVID-19 on the cruise industry, and on so many others worldwide, was like sailing into and through a very dense fog. COVID is a river of fog that just keeps coming.

I know what it's like to feel lost. And if there's one thing I already know about you, it's that you do too. That's the reason you picked up this book. You're in the thick of it, whether it's the fog of a pandemic, a disruption to your industry or career, or a personal crisis such as a sudden job loss. The world as you know it has changed; you're not sure what to do about it; and possibly, you can't see forward, backward, or any way out.

Dealing with this most recent disruption is a momentous task. If you can not only recover from it but also find a way to use the experience for good, you'll be ready for anything. As my cruise colleagues and I navigate our industry through COVID-19, we don't make wild guesses; we rely on a proven framework for survival, stability, and success. We also need a dose of humility. We would not have made it without mass vaccination. Before coronavirus, the record for the fastest vaccine development—for mumps—was four years. Most vaccines have required more than a decade of research and experimentation. The cruise, travel, and tourism industry can endure a year of critical disruption but not four years of lockdowns. Thankfully, collaboration between national governments and private pharmaceutical companies broke the previous record. Healing is coming.

Even as the cruise industry is in the very beginning and uncertain stages of emerging from the coronavirus pandemic, I'm acutely aware this isn't our first rodeo. I've also helped companies and the industry manage through other major catastrophes, incidents, and setbacks, going back to the *Achille Lauro* hijacking in 1985, the first Gulf War in 1990 and encompassing 9/11, SARS-1, Gulf War II, the global financial crisis, the H1N1 pandemic (swine flu), the *Costa Concordia* disaster, the European refugee crisis, and now this—COVID-19, the industry's greatest challenge yet.

If people know there's a war going on somewhere, the tourism industry is greatly affected. People want to stay close to home. They're less adventurous. The Gulf Wars made people hesitant to travel internationally, and many canceled their vacations. One benefit of cruise ships is they can be moved and relocated to other locations in the world, unlike hotels and resorts. Cruise companies can reposition ships and capacity to areas where people still want to travel. Even so, there is significant and lasting financial impact involved in making such changes to global deployment plans and operations already underway.

Fast forward a decade to September 2001. September 11 had long-lasting effects on travel, even though it happened suddenly on a single day. It most greatly affected air travel, but people initially could not get to the ships, and many didn't feel safe traveling at all; 9/11 was more emotionally terrifying. The impact on the cruise industry wasn't as long lasting, but it was deep nonetheless. I wrote the following journal entry on December 31, 2001: "The last day of a tough year. But I think the lesson of 2001 was that anything can happen, life and security are fragile, time marches on, people rise to the occasion, we are very fortunate to live in America."

In retrospect, it felt like a preview of SARS-1. That outbreak really only disrupted a corner of the world, but it made everyone more cautious. SARS wasn't found on cruise ships, and so it was, of course, less severe than COVID-19. The COVID-19 outbreaks on cruise ships created very graphic, negative publicity for the cruise industry worldwide. The world saw people stuck in quarantine on cruise ships, front and center on the news and on social media continuously for weeks. SARS-1 was much smaller in scope and affected airlines more than cruise ships.

The second Gulf War complicated tourism, and the great recession slowed growth substantially. Fear and uncertainty reached all-time highs. An economic downturn more severe than anything since the Great Depression made things a struggle to say the least. The mood and trepidation of that decade are apparent in my journal entry from January 1, 2006:

> Life is definitely an experience of walking on the edge, doing one's best to maintain equilibrium—and to regain it as quickly as possible whenever we fall off, or get knocked off, our precarious perch. Sometimes regaining our position is achieved by redefining our perspective. Changing our rules. Determination, courage, and flexibility are required.

The great recession was preceded by the bursting of the dot-com bubble, both of which affected the ability of many travelers to make discretionary expenditures, including vacations and cruises. Other industry-shaking events (as well as a few personal trials) have provided important lessons on making it through the fog. Over the years, I have shared these lessons with employees, in speeches, at events, and on

CHAPTER 1 - INTO THE FOG

LinkedIn. I may not have been an actual captain on a cruise ship, but I was certainly the equivalent in the executive ranks on shore, directing company-wide responses to, and recovery from, all manner of disruptions. If ever there was a time to put these lessons on paper for you to learn from, it's now.

How do you know what I have to say will be useful? I have a proven track record in (and a passion for) helping innovative companies and organizations in the cruise and tourism industry achieve results, identify new opportunities, and uniquely position themselves for future success.

I've worked alongside some of the top consulting firms in the world—having either hired them, served as an expert resource, or worked collaboratively to address challenges and unearth opportunities within client companies. I have also collaborated with investment funds on investments and potential investments in the cruise and travel industry.

I didn't come this far to only go this far. I made it a policy early on that I would always make myself available to others. I believe in karma, and I get as much as I give. I decided to write this book for anyone who needs inspiration so I can share what inspired the individuals I've worked with. I'm also at the point in my life when I'm thinking deeply about new ways of contributing. Part of that legacy is packaging what I've learned from clients and companies and what they've learned from me into a manual anyone can use to navigate through the fog.

When disruption envelops us, there is so much information to gather. So many sources and points of view, all inconsistent with one another. But very few conclusions. Are there any conclusions you are so confident in the quality of information and the process and experience behind them that you can bank on? Not yet?

Here are mine, and yes, you can bank on them. This is my playbook. My nautical chart to guide you through and out of the fog with the ship of your soul intact. What will you find in these pages? I'll share stories of how I've endured disruption—packed with deep knowledge, steady leadership, and practical advice. Why lessons from the cruise industry? Well, what works for us definitely works for any organization, industry, or individual because no organization, industry, or individual has it as tough as we do most of the time. Everything is intertwined and intensive, meaning there is no such thing as low-risk anything in this business. It's not like an internet business you can start up or shut down or a freelance service you sometimes offer or promote as needed or scale up by hiring subcontractors on demand. We are capital intensive, operations intensive, regulation intensive, place intensive (e.g., ports, islands, etc.), infrastructure intensive, employee intensive (e.g., recruiting and training), and marketing and distribution intensive.

If something works for us, it works for anyone. That's why this book offers advice to a broader audience beyond travel executives and investors. It helps anyone whose job, business, investment, or private life faces disruption. And these lessons aren't only about the cruise industry. I've got multi-industry experience surviving and thriving during disruption—from market panics and viral pandemics to terrorism and trade wars.

With decades of experience seeing the world through the lens of some of the hardest-hit industries, I am not simply teaching you *what* to do but rather showing you how to *think* about what to do. A holistic approach, including customer care, preservation of jobs and talent pool, core constituents connected in new ways, strategic thinking, financial resourcefulness, marketing communications, and distribution channels, applies to all industries.

In the fog, fear skews our memory of the fundamentals. We're clouded by emotion and feel disoriented. You already know this, but you probably haven't applied it to these conditions we see today. It's hard to make even easy decisions when you can't tell the difference between safe and unsafe. The fundamentals never change, but the feelings about the situation do—as do the risks of making the wrong choice. Sometimes you set sail in sunny weather, but a storm comes in that knocks you off course. This book will be your guide through that storm and out of the fog.

Fortunately, at the time of this writing, the fog of the pandemic has begun to lift. The cruise and travel industry was literally saved by the vaccine. We could endure a year of critical disruption, but not four years—the previous vaccine record for mumps—much less for decades, the normal time line for vaccines.

The day our tides turned will go down in history as December 15, 2020, as the *New York Times* reported:

> Before COVID-19, the record for the fastest vaccine development—for mumps—was four years. Most vaccines have required more than a decade of research and experimentation.
>
> Yet yesterday morning, less than a year after the discovery of COVID, a critical care nurse in Queens named Sandra Lindsay became the first American to participate in the mass vaccination program for the coronavirus. "I feel like healing is coming," she said afterward.[2]

It is a stunning story of scientific success.

As with every disruption, there has been much to learn. A chief lesson for me was that the time to write this book had come. Initially, I did plan to write this book exclusively for the cruise industry. An article I wrote recently called "An Updated Look at the Expedition/Adventure Cruise Market" laid out six imperatives for cruise industry recovery, all specific to cruise companies. But the more I discussed them with clients, friends, and even family, the more I realized that these imperatives have a much broader application—even beyond the coronavirus. They apply equally to global disruption and to personal events. Everything I've learned and shared with clients over the decades is bound up in these six imperatives. If the status quo has changed, everything else has with it—your priorities, your concerns, and your vision for the future. To paraphrase Marshall Goldsmith, what brought you into the fog won't get you out of it.

---

2   David Leonhardt, "Good morning. The Covid Vaccine Is Here, and We Explain How It Arrived with Stunning Speed," *New York Times*, December 15, 2020, https://messaging-custom-newsletters.nytimes.com/template/oakv2?abVariantId=3&-campaign_id=9&emc=edit_nn_20201215&instance_id=25050&nl=the-morning&productCode=NN&regi_id=65869109&segment_id=46979&te=1&uri=ny-t%3A%2F%2Fnewsletter%2F20eab231-3a67-5e1c-ab7d-a6bcd5b94047&user_id=5a892e516000dd81af66b6e7f427fcde.

For the purposes of this book, I've renamed the six imperatives the six protocols for survival, stability, and success. A protocol is a best practice we follow faithfully, skipping it at our own peril. Just as there are specific protocols to follow when the fog rolls in, so, too, are there equivalent protocols for business, for your job, and for life.

The increasing rate of change, the speed of commerce, and the frequency of disruptions are a reality. Your ability to move through it, adapt, and repurpose is the key to sustained success. The six protocols will help you do just that, even as they enable you to make it through disruption safely.

The Six Protocols for Survival, Stability, and Success

1. **Know your waypoint**: Where exactly were you when the disruption happened? When you're in the fog, you need as much information as possible, including which type of disruption you're facing. (Yes, there are more than one.)
2. **Stay afloat**: How many resources do you need to outlast the disruption? Cash is the fuel that powers your ship through unknown waters. Get and keep as much as possible to keep from sinking.
3. **Find your first first**: What is the one thing that, if lost during the disruption, makes recovery impossible? Identify and plan everything around that.
4. **Get flexible**: Everything has changed, so you should too. What does recovery look like? How can you make the most of your time in the fog and position yourself to come out flying your flag higher than ever before?
5. **Become collision proof**: How do you make yourself anti-fragile? The old saying goes that we're always either going into a disruption, actively in one, or just coming out of one.

Some collisions with the most devastating parts of disruption can be avoided. You'll need to survive the ones that can't.

6. **Protect your value**: How do you protect your time, effort, and worth when the world around you is falling apart, panicking, or discounting everything of value? This protocol also applies to pricing when consumers are reluctant to buy and to our own self-confidence.

Wherever you find yourself, and whatever is going on in the world, these protocols will lead you to recovery, no matter what situation you face. Together, we'll go through them one by one, and you'll have them here as a playbook to refer back to—and that's exactly how you should use this book. You have my permission to skip to the sections that are relevant to your situation right now. Whether you're earning your living through a day job or leading an entire enterprise, at least one of these protocols will speak to your current situation. Before you know it, one of the other five will as well. That's when you should dive into them most—when you know you need them.

As you read this book, you'll be following footprints into the future. I first used that term in a June 2002 journal entry. Here it is:

Today I thought about the new project and understood it as a Footprint in the Future. I realized that anybody can have plans, but until you make a tangible commitment, a "footprint" in that future, you have no chance of realizing the dream.

Let me make one thing clear. These protocols are not about getting back to normal. They're about getting on board with the *new* normal—the way things are going to be from now on. When you embrace the change instead of fighting against it, you start putting footprints in the future. The promise of this book is to get you out of the fog so you can sail again with fair winds and following seas.

You can make a footprint in the future right now. Make a commitment to yourself to read this entire book and use all the tools as they apply to you. Our economy is at a chasm, and we must all find our way across it. You know you can't cross it in one step. Instead, you focus on getting one foot planted on the other side, and then you use that momentum to pull the rest of your body across. It's that physical act of committing energy and direction in the future that creates that first footprint. By doing the things recommended in this book, you'll be taking a mental and emotional journey across the chasm.

Yes, I'm keeping the chasm metaphor. I grew up in Alaska, America's home of glaciers. Many times, I walked right up to the edge of one of those deep, terrifying chasms. The ones where, if you slipped, you'd never be found. At the bottom of those glacial fissures are massive rivers. You can hear them roaring like monsters below. This glacial melt is what shapes the earth, carving into the rock. You can't stop the chasm, nor should you want to. With your foot firmly planted in the future, you won't fall in.

It's time to stop chasing the past and become as clear-eyed as possible about the future. Do not rely on and return to old familiar metrics. You'll do yourself a great disservice with "But this is the way it's supposed to work." While there are six protocols that will navigate you through disruption, there is only one mindset: I accept what is difficult. The six protocols are not easy. But it's better to survive, get stable, and chart your new course to success than it is to give up.

If you're ready, the six protocols are docked and ready for you.

One foot first.

CHAPTER 2

Know Your Waypoint

The First Protocol for Survival, Stability, and Success

Not all storms come to disrupt your life. Some come to clear your path.

—Anonymous

It is stunning and surreal.

I journaled that sentence when the world entered the COVID-19 scare. Either by reading the last chapter or by living it, you know how enormous the disruption was. Stock markets plunged to their lowest point in nearly four decades. Over half a million businesses in North America alone shuttered for good. The United States government sent the country's first-ever universal basic income checks to the majority of citizens in hopes of tiding us over as we waited "fifteen days to slow the spread." What an extraordinary time.

Fifteen days became fifteen weeks. Would the shutdowns and lock-downs last fifteen months? Longer? No one knew. We all did our best to adjust to the new normal. Office towers emptied, with everyone either laid off or working from home. Downtown cores of major cities and freeways throughout the states had little to no traffic. Restaurants and bars closed. Citizens were advised (and in some cases ordered) to maintain social distancing, restrict movements outside the home, or shelter in place. All events and group gatherings of any kind were canceled. It was, in fact, stunning and surreal.

Great financial damage accrued not only in the stock market but also in many companies, large and small. The economic ramifications had only just begun to be considered. Coronavirus plagued the travel industry like no other. Over half of all airplanes were grounded. Most hotels were closed and empty. A few served as makeshift quarantine centers. Global cruising saw our industry's entire fleet of 314 ships laid up and anchored at ports around the world. Although in some ways, travel would become safer and healthier, it would certainly never be the same. In many respects, the coronavirus shutdown was as bizarre and far-reaching as the terrorist attacks of September 11, 2001: deep impact and disruption followed by long-term changes in daily life. For me personally, as with so many other businesses, my client projects and payments were interrupted and delayed.

Think for a moment of the incredible years of work and investment required to design and build world-class cruise travel experiences. From construction of the ships themselves to designing the itineraries; providing onboard amenities, skilled officers and crew members, services, and entertainment; and planning exciting shore-based experiences at every stop. Then to make them viable and successful in the marketplace requires brand positioning, marketing, communications, distribution, sales, reservations, inventory, and yield management, all costing tens of billions of dollars. Suddenly, much of that had to be not only halted but also unwound. Revenues not only stopped but were also reversed in the form of refunds.

Many expenses and critical responsibilities remained. Tens of thousands of crew members were unable to return home after the ships ceased operations. Travel restrictions and international disputes left them in a position of great uncertainty. The ships that were their place of work became islands on which they found themselves as stranded castaways. The cruise lines had no more sacred duty than to address the health, well-being, and repatriating of their valued crew members. The logistics of winding down operations while maintaining assets and core headquarters functions worldwide involved a great amount of expense. Major cruise lines experienced a nonoperating cash burn rate collectively of $2 billion per month!

We hadn't even begun to consider the full effect of nonoperating expenses for a period of several months or how to go about restarting the engine in this new reality. The cash and capital requirements of restarting would be enormous. How would smaller brands survive this leg of the journey? How big a journey of change and recovery were we even looking at?

Wave after wave of new infections and hospitalizations, many including coworkers, friends, and family, made another fifteen months of uncertainty feel inevitable. Still, we hoped the worst would pass by the end of 2020. The world and all of us in it needed to get back to work. From Fortune 500 executives to interns at startups, the world's employees would never take job security and economic stability for granted again.

Even as restaurants and bars reopened with reduced capacity and other organizations went back to work with new safety measures in place, the cruise industry remained locked in the doldrums. It was as though we were dead in the water with no propulsion or steerage and no one coming to our rescue. No financial lifeline was thrown to the cruise industry in the unprecedented government rescue funds for businesses and individuals. The cruise companies would have to pick up the pieces and put them back together themselves. Cruise executives began planning ways to restart and rebuild. New science and new protocols to address new regulations and overcome new restrictions. The cruise industry was held to a higher standard in light of the unfortunate incidents involving cruise ships in the early days of COVID's appearance. How would the industry keep its head above water and begin moving forward out of the situation?

It turns out I have more experience at that than I'd like to admit. Fighting back. Dealing with disruption and defining a route to recovery. My experience and expertise in cruise business development, management, and marketing when the economy collapses or world events threaten are what people often look to me for. I've seen plenty of it. While cruise ships were being laid up for an undefined period of time, I got busy very quickly. There were some unforeseen opportunities for cruise companies, and they were desperate to find and assemble them into something resembling cash flow. The same can be said for any industry. But we can only find them if we hold on and focus forward through these unprecedented circumstances.

While the world—and the cruise industry—paused, I never stopped. Neither did the cruise industry behind the scenes. During COVID-19, I helped a large private equity firm–backed group of companies acquire and integrate a supplier important to the company's longer-term product development and delivery and then identify and acquire similar companies. Creating synergies and identifying high-performance best practices and technologies that will accelerate future multiples of value.

I've also helped position a technology platform in travel distribution to catch the opportunity wave created by enormous disruption. And I'm helping bring the best kind of cruise travel back to the world with new market approaches including "Where Will You Be When the World Reopens?" a provocative challenge to adventure travelers, and "Come Home to America in 2021," an invitation to rediscover the nearby and familiar while taking those first steps toward venturing out again. At the same time, I'm helping save and create jobs and define future value opportunities for company owners and senior management teams. This is my higher purpose in this difficult time in the industry.

One cruise industry CEO I worked with amid the COVID turmoil is also an innovator and founder of an amazing cruise company that operates a small fleet of unique ships providing a combination of river, coastal, and expedition cruises. While not one of the giant companies in the cruise industry, this particular cruise line is substantial and offers unique experiences, with a successful bottom line. The cruises serve older, experienced travelers with voyages that deeply immerse guests in off-the-beaten-track destinations, featuring history, culture, nature, and local flavors.

When the authorities quarantined the *Diamond Princess*, the first ship struck by COVID, like other executives, my client was rightly concerned about the future of the industry and his company. He didn't know how bad COVID would be. No one did. Every day the ships didn't operate, they lost money and burned precious cash reserves. The shutdowns were nothing less than the inverse of a big bang. A reverse expansion—a mega-contraction—occurred, shrinking a multibillion-dollar industry into nothing overnight. No cruise industry contingency plans included a section on what to do when the industry with $45 billion in annual revenues plummets to an annualized loss of $25 billion and a cumulative decline in stock market value among the big three of $65 billion between January and April 2020.

As the reality of the situation sunk in, we shifted into crisis management mode. *If it's going to get bad, let's not make it worse.* Prior to the pandemic, cruise executives saw their jobs as orchestrating each customer's perfect cruise experience, optimizing financial results, building a high-performance culture and a talented team of employees, coordinating the objectives of multiple stakeholders, and providing vision and direction for continued growth and success. But with everything grinding to a halt, leadership was torn between relieving cruise guests' fears about ever sailing again and swiftly reversing the negative revenue trend to preserve their companies and tens of thousands of valued employees.

When the first ban on cruise ships took effect in March 2020, we had to get a handle on the fact that we were canceling cruises for the next four weeks. That meant notifying all guests, some who were en route, and confirming plans to resume cruises in mid- to late April. However, health and safety regulations extended the cancellations for another four weeks, then another. By the time it was necessary to cancel a series of future cruises a third time, companies were stuck between holding on to hope that this would be the last set of revisions and concern that the COVID situation appeared to be getting worse across the board.

"I'm worried I'm not doing the right thing," one client told me. "Or if I am doing the right thing, I'm not doing enough of it."

Together with the talented senior management team, we worked through the upended status quo. We chose to do the opposite of nothing. To be the opposite of helpless. Because doing nothing was a sinkhole, a continuing loss of traction and position with a worsening set of options. In just twenty weeks, we regained control of the company's trajectory, turned it forward, and advanced their position significantly through cash gains and future revenue gains in the form of new bookings and deposits. They were now positioned solidly for continued forward progress at an even faster pace.

One of the unique aspects of cruise and travel—and one of the things I most enjoy—is that we're in the people business. It's people providing service and delivering life-changing experiences for other people. Leaders in this business are emotionally invested. It's not the ships we're most attached to; it's the experiences that guests have aboard those ships. We must not only manage our own emotions around the disruption but also redirect the tangible fears of thousands of employees, guests, and other stakeholders. We must find and create hope and share it with everyone else.

The first advice I gave clients about responding to the coronavirus or any other disruption was to start with their waypoint, which is what you're going to do in this chapter. In a seafaring context, knowing your waypoint means you have gathered information based on where you are at that moment and what you know. What other vessels are in the vicinity? Where is the shoreline? Are there shoals or shallows to avoid? What's your speed? Where are you going? The moment that fog rolls in, it can be overwhelming. You recalibrate by pulling together a realistic assessment from which to make decisions.

Proceed headlong into disruption without mapping it, and you imperil yourself and others. The very same week that the coronavirus outbreak went full pandemic, professional basketball legend Kobe Bryant perished in a helicopter crash along with nine others, including his daughter. A year later, the National Transportation Safety Board discovered why—the pilot was trying to climb above the clouds while he was actually rapidly falling, a sure sign of disorientation.[3] The right thing but the wrong direction.

At the first sign of disruption, slow up. Hold if necessary. Get oriented. Stay engaged and vigilant. Then do the opposite of nothing . . . very slowly.

When the first ships got quarantined, my advice was to slow down and regroup. Put everything we know about our waypoint on paper. We needed a system through which to think about and approach the many decisions and actions ahead.

Here is an example of an email I sent to a client in mid-March 2020.

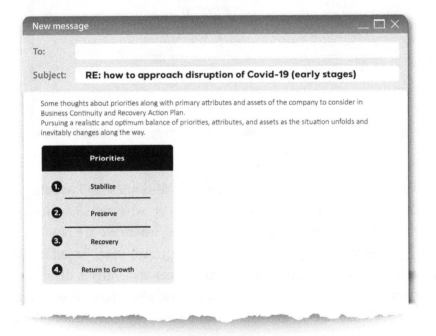

---

3   "Investigators Fault Pilot in Kobe Bryant Crash for Flying into Clouds," *New York Times*, February 9, 2021, www.nytimes.com/2021/02/09/us/kobe-helicopter-crash-investigation.html?campaign_id=60&emc=edit_na_20210209&instance_id=0&nl=breaking-news&ref=cta&regi_id=65869109&segment_id=51287&user_id=5a892e516000dd81af66b6e7f427fcde.

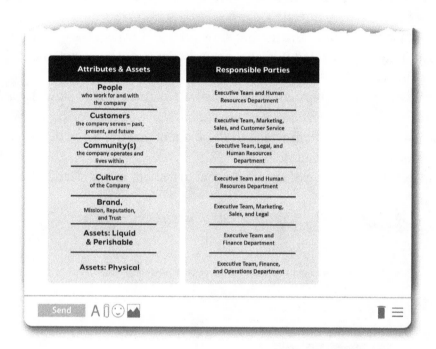

Attributes & Assets	Responsible Parties
People who work for and with the company	Executive Team and Human Resources Department
Customers the company serves – past, present, and future	Executive Team, Marketing, Sales, and Customer Service
Community(s) the company operates and lives within	Executive Team, Legal, and Human Resources Department
Culture of the Company	Executive Team and Human Resources Department
Brand, Mission, Reputation, and Trust	Executive Team, Marketing, Sales, and Legal
Assets: Liquid & Perishable	Executive Team and Finance Department
Assets: Physical	Executive Team, Finance, and Operations Department

This simple framework of priorities, attributes and assets, and responsible parties offered a way to inventory what we *did* know. We can only decide where to go next by defining where we are now.

If you look closely at this framework, you'll see I break down a cruise company into manageable components. I identify a detailed list of affected assets and whose job it is to look after them. People come first for obvious reasons, just as they would in every case. Assets, though valuable, can be repaired or replaced. Without committed and passionate employees and loyal, trusting customers, your business and your livelihood are gone.

I advised companies to view their employees through this fog navigation chart. What kind of messaging do they need while going through a trauma like this? What support can be given? And what is the impact, especially for those who will be furloughed, see their salaries cut, or lose their jobs no matter what we do?

The next priority to consider was how customers (past, present, and future) were affected by this event. And then the broader communities the company engaged with, as well as the culture and brand of the company and its various types of assets. We used this framework to map the unknown territory.

The point of sharing this framework with you is that we didn't know how bad it was going to get. But we knew we had to start somewhere— with what we *did* know. For my clients, my own company, or anyone facing disruption in their personal life, business, career, or industry, knowing your waypoint means facing where you were when it happened. That's where you'll start to figure out where you're going next. Over the course of this chapter, we'll be mapping your precise location when the disruption began—your precise waypoint.

This is what I did myself and how I've helped other executives and investors during the pandemic and during previous disruptions. When you know what absolutely has to get done no matter what, what those priorities affect, and who is responsible for them, you have yourself the beginnings of a plan.

We'll return to the navigation chart later in this chapter. For now, we're going to study what goes into your personal framework. What are *your* attributes, assets, and responsible parties? Just as importantly, how do you map them all out when you feel like curling up on the floor in a pool of your own tears? Your priorities are likely the same as a cruise industry CEO's—stabilize the situation, preserve what you currently have, recover from the disruption's consequences, and return to growth.

But knowing that you have these priorities doesn't tell you how to follow them. Hypothetical knowledge is not enough. Not for running a business, not for real life. You're here for actionable advice. Here it is.

What You Need to Know to Know Your Waypoint

You know those shopping mall maps that tell you "You Are Here" so you can quickly find your way around a maze of shops to your desired destination? The navigation chart you're building is something like that. It only works as intended if the "You Are Here" waypoint is present on the map. Knowing that disruption is happening without knowing your place in it is the worst-case scenario.

What follows here are several tips that will collectively enable you to create your own navigation chart. Except yours will be tailored to the exact disruption you're experiencing right now: personal, professional, global, or otherwise.

To create your own navigation chart to find your way through the fog, there are several things you must know and do. This is critical to your ability to move forward consistently and cautiously. To move in the direction of recovery at all times.

Give Yourself a Reality Check

In 1849, French novelist Jean-Baptiste Alphonse Karr wrote, "*Plus ça change, plus c'est la même chose.*" You may recognize the more common English translation: "The more things change, the more they stay the same."

Most people follow this advice when they encounter disruption. The best thing to do when entering the fog, they reason, is to stay the course. Through all the disruptions I've navigated in cruising, in other industries, and in my personal life, and through helping others do the same, I've learned the truth about this cliché. It's dangerously full of holes.

First of all, maybe you *should* keep to the same course as before. But most likely not. When the status quo changes, the dreams, goals, and plans you drew up based on your previous situation are made obsolete. That's what disruption does. Because priorities change. For the cruise industry, the situation went from "managing growth" to "mitigating disaster." Those waypoints could not be more different.

The second reason Karr's quote sinks people deeper into disruption is its false sense of security. *Stick to the plan . . . everything will be OK.* In companies, this manifests in leadership doubling down on next quarter's objectives or the annual vision. In the face of disruption, this isn't helpful.

Charting our waypoint requires us to separate facts from previous assumptions and even wishes. This is incredibly difficult because it requires, as I tell clients, "throwing out the old playbook." Thus, staying the course when the course is no longer visible is increasingly fraught with danger. The farther you proceed into the fog, the greater the risk that you'll collide with peril. The sooner we let go of the way things have always been done, the sooner we can get to answering the question behind the first protocol: "This is stunning and surreal. So now what?"

The sudden COVID-19 operational halt was an unimaginable setback for even the best-positioned companies. There was a heavy focus on the circumstances and outlook of the mainstream cruise lines, but there was little discussion about the unique challenges facing specialized operators such as river cruise companies or small ship and expedition cruise companies. The business trajectory was progressing differently now because of new market realities and operating conditions, which is why no one could stay the course. Companies of all types were challenged to adapt. While we could anticipate new consumer preferences for small ships and uncrowded destinations, there were big problems in staying afloat financially and operationally.

This brings us back to avoiding assumptions and focusing on what we know about where we are.

Get All the Bad News Out of the Way

The most useful questions to ask as soon as disruption occurs are "How big is it, and how bad is it?" It helps you see things clear-eyed and get past the emotion. You may have a strong desire to resist the changes you are facing and be determined to get back on course quickly. Those are good things to have to get through a disruption. They just have to be harnessed in service of a clear understanding of where you're really at.

When you're surrounded by fog and you realize you can't see anything, that's the moment you must stop everything and take stock of what you know. To plan present and future moves, you need any and all information available. That includes information you may not want to hear. So get all the bad news out of the way as soon as you can. What challenge is right in front of you? Is there an even more defining one? Are you being reactive? Or are you relying on full and complete information to understand the forces at play?

I'm an information sponge. There's a point at which I get waterlogged. There comes a point in information gathering when you're procrastinating. Too much information becomes less actionable. Imagine an upside-down triangle: there's a point at which there's enough information to take large action, but after that, more information doesn't necessarily incrementally improve action.

How do you know when enough is enough? When you have no new questions to ask, you no longer get a return on research.

Once you have a good idea about what the disruption means for your organization, your career, or your life, you can work your way forward from there.

Discern Which Type of Disruption You're Facing

Perhaps the most important information you need to know is the exact type of disruption you've just found yourself in. Is it a slow and steady compression that increasingly threatens the viability and security of your company or career over time? Or was there a sudden explosive jolt that threw everything into peril? Both can happen, yet each requires a different response. Knowing the nuances of each disruption type helps you better prepare for what's next so you can quickly act.

Sudden Jolt Disruptions

These disruptions derail everything all at once. We're left wondering what the hell just happened. The cruise industry has endured quite a few of these over the last three decades, as have I personally.

In 1991, the Persian Gulf War between the United States and Iraq was small and localized from a combat perspective. Still, there was considerable disruption in cruise vacations and airline travel. We saw global impacts on both for a short duration.[4] I came to fully realize the lack of geographical knowledge among many vacation travelers. A Western Mediterranean cruise was not even remotely close to the military actions in the Middle East. But for many Americans, there was no geographic distinction. It was all the Eastern Hemisphere—"over there"—thus, sudden cancellations affected summer cruise plans. At Windstar Cruises, I had to make the decision to redeploy our vessels out of the Mediterranean and regroup with cruises in the Bahamas and Alaska instead. Very impactful, to say the least. What was even more significant was the increase in oil prices due to the unrest in the region. Cruise companies had to implement fuel surcharges in response. Still, once the transportation and travel industries survived the big wave of change, we made plans to turn things around. And we did. That doesn't mean it wasn't costly, but we made it through yet again. If you are experiencing a sudden jolt disruption, expect its impact to show up in places and ways you did not expect.

Fast forward ten years. The attacks on September 11, 2001, were severe and restrictive immediately and then lessened moving forward. There was a 9/11 but not a 9/12. While the immediate effects of 9/11 were sudden, it began a decade of further disruption. Permanent improvements in security changed the industry to a certain degree but not in an overly restrictive way. Still, there were noticeable changes in daily life that exist to this day. Sometimes, there is no going back to

---

4   Evelyn Thomchick, "The 1991 Persian Gulf War: Short-Term Impacts on Ocean and Air Transportation," *Transportation Journal* 33, no. 2 (1993): 40–53, www.jstor.org/stable/20713195.

normal. You are better off looking toward a new normal than reminiscing about the good old days. This is the more productive way to view the fallout—even when tragedy occurs.

I've personally experienced no shortage of those. Only a few short days after 9/11, while we were reeling from the incident, at Holland America Line, we faced another tragedy when a number of guests aboard one of our ships perished in a small airplane crash during a shore excursion in Mexico that killed all nineteen on board. This tragedy was made all the more difficult by the fact that sixteen passengers were alumni of the University of Washington and members of the community where the company was headquartered. I will never forget that night or participating in the calls to notify families of the deceased or the crush of the media. Everyone was still reeling from the hijacked airliner attacks on the country. Yet this plane crash was caused by engine failure, not terrorism. An investigation ensued, resulting in stricter regulations and an increased awareness of shore excursion safety procedures. Expect sudden unexpected disruptions of all types to change "the way we do things" immediately and forever.

A more widely known travel incident was the *Costa Concordia* disaster. In 2012, a luxury cruise liner struck a rock in shallow waters off the Italian coast. Thirty-three souls perished, including twenty-seven guests. The public was shocked by the suddenness of the tragedy. For the cruise industry, the disruption was immediate as the death toll and human error involved raised serious questions and concerns. Trust was lost; people were generally more hesitant to cruise. The entire industry felt the financial consequences but none as intensely as the cruise company, Costa Crociere. The disruption's total cost, including victims' compensation and refloating, towing, and scrapping the ship, was $2 billion. The ship's construction itself cost only $612 million. A full accounting of the consequences of sudden disruption is often much greater than expected. And you likely have only heartache and setback to show for it. Acknowledge this, and you'll be able to manage just about any emotion as you recover from disruption.

Personal disruptions are often the most unexpected and far-reaching. I faced my biggest disruption in my thirties. I had built an Alaska cruise and tour business with my family that expanded its fleet of ships and operations to destinations around the world: Tahiti, Panama, Costa Rica, Baja's Sea of Cortez, the Caribbean, Eastern Canada, and Europe. We'd innovated, grown, and operated for more than a decade. We worked hard and built the business from the ground up. My children were young, and that was how I supported them. Both my parents and my sister worked in the business with me and hundreds of wonderful employees. At the time, it was everything in my life.

A large company approached us with an offer for a majority ownership purchase. We ultimately agreed. That capital infusion enabled us to continue to expand operations rapidly. For a family business self-financed and bootstrapped, access to financial capital and resources was transformative. It was an exciting time, and we had high hopes for the partnership. Then unexpectedly, the majority shareholder changed course and pulled the plug on our life's work. A financial rounding error for them, a catastrophe for our company. We spent years in court. It felt insurmountable. My entire identity and all my financial entanglements were wrapped up in this disruption. A merger of family and business with no boundaries can be a challenge, even at the best of times. We were selling assets to pay legal fees, but the company ultimately didn't survive. We fought hard to make it work, and we still lost everything. The only thing we could do was to turn our focus to the future and our next plan of action. Even a disappointing failure does not end your options for overcoming disruption successfully.

In the end, I learned a painful lesson that was further strengthened by my ability to adapt. It also ended up opening doors for me into the multibillion-dollar global cruise industry. One key takeaway from my experience was to write down my waypoint on paper—in my case, journaling—so I could begin to see where I was and where I needed to go. It doesn't matter how bad it is. If you hit rock bottom, you'll find the core of the problem. Instead of avoiding it, be willing to do the work to recover. In the midst of deep personal disruption, I noted in my journal, "My life is rich and full. The good and the bad are all the same—the stuff of life."

Slow Leak Disruptions

The second type of disruptions are protracted. They begin with an onset, but they build and worsen over time. COVID-19 is the biggest example yet of this type of disruption faced by the global cruise industry. If nobody knew it would get this big or this bad, that's a slow leak disruption. It may not seem like it at first, but the longer it goes on, the more likely your plans, your goals, your hopes, and your dreams slow to a halt, begin to drift, and slide backward at an increasing speed.

In 2008, the bankruptcy of major financial lenders in the United States had a ripple effect on economies worldwide. The global economic downturn slowed travel as people were faced with foreclosure, rising costs, and less available credit.[5] This financial crisis took place over the course of multiple years, and while some saw it coming, no one expected it to cause such wide-reaching disruptions. Still, the cruise industry regrouped and continued to grow by focusing on more affordable itineraries, moving ships to operate closer to key population centers, offering lower prices, and including more value in order to compete aggressively for every possible vacation dollar. We did this by figuring out exactly where we were and where the market was headed so we could chart our course out. You can do the same.

The emergence of COVID-19 and the resulting long-term global disruption initially came on slowly, to the point where people didn't know how to react or what to expect. Since it had a slower onset, the risk was not fully realized initially as no one anticipated the long-term effects on people, the economy, and the world. The cruise industry was scrambling to regain its footing, with no realization that we were in it for the long haul. Companies were faced with a temporary shutdown, something that was previously unheard of and economically devastating. With disruptions that are slow in coming, we can often adapt as they unfold, especially if we are productive and paying attention.

---

5   Martha Brannigan, "Cruise Industry Aims to Navigate Through Recession," *Miami Herald*, last modified June 15, 2015, www.mcclatchydc.com/news/nation-world/national/economy/article24529840.html.

There are many other slow-onset disruptions that can happen to a specific region, an organization, or an individual. One example of this is a slow slide into irrelevance, accelerated by an aggressive and innovative competitor. For example, one cruise line I worked with several years ago retained their longstanding brand as an old-world cruise. Traditional. Formal. Worldly. Built by and for our parents' parents. A "Tradition of Excellence" was the company promise. But over time, market forces changed. New, more contemporary competitors disrupted their market share. The company didn't know how to adapt because they were focused on a rigorous commitment to the traditional cruise experience. I led the company's response and recovery strategy from this powerful marketplace disruption. We shifted dramatically from a "Tradition of Excellence" to a "Signature of Excellence," backed up by several hundred million dollars of investments in new ship designs, itineraries, culinary experiences, activities and services, and marketing repositioning that appealed to the sensibilities of a new generation of travelers.

Disruption is not just how it starts, how long it lasts, or how bad it is; it's how it ends. During slower, longer-lasting disruptions, expect things to go from bad to worse. Watch for the final snap of the tail, when the stored energy of the disruption event makes its final concentrated burst, and many of those who managed to barely hang on until this point but are weakened finally lose their grip and are tossed aside entirely. It's the point at which struggling businesses, unable to adapt or secure resources, fail. It is the point at which careers that also fail to adapt and innovate are ended. In some cases, the snap is more like a ripple effect.

In 2021, the snap of COVID's tail hurt Canada and Alaska with the sharpest of pain. Just when the start of the recovery appeared on the horizon, when the cruise, travel, and tourism industry's endurance and resources were strained to their final limit, we felt the snap. On February 4, just over one full year into the pandemic, Canada announced the closure of all cruise ports for another year, effectively ending hope of a summer cruise season in Alaska, eastern Canada, and the Canadian Arctic. Bad news for cruise lines. Devastating news for the small communities, businesses, and thousands of employees dependent on tourism in Alaska and Canada. This would be the second missed summer. Two full seasons of loss and hardship. And a long wait for the next summer season.

Then on February 7, 2021, the *New York Times* reported that a new strain of COVID-19 first discovered in the UK had found its way to the United States.[6] Reports suggest this new strain is almost half again as contagious as the first strain, and experts expect it to replace the previous strain as the most dominant in both nations.

The snap. It's brutal. And that's an understatement. If you are to have any chance of outlasting whatever you face, I want you prepared for how bad it can be. And that's pretty bad. An endurance mindset, nimble flexibility, and relentless vigilance are required in these circumstances.

Getting real with yourself about the disruption, learning as much about it as you can, and figuring out which type of disruption you're facing are all key to mapping your waypoint. But before you can complete your own navigation chart to plan your course through the fog, we must address one more variable: you.

Consider Your Momentum

Disruption brings uncertainty. Uncertainty triggers questions. *Should I hold my current position? Should I change course? Should I continue full speed ahead? Or is a combination required?* Sometimes you just wait. The disruption is prolonged and deep. You do everything you can in your power and in collaboration with others, and then . . . you wait. Like waiting to be rescued from a deserted island or when lost at sea.

When you are faced with disruption, consider how it affects your momentum. What course were you following when the event appeared? What trajectory were you on, and how far would that momentum carry you along that original path if not altered or adjusted? What was the most recent waypoint on your charted course, and what is the next one

6   Carl Zimmer, "Virus Variant First Found in Britain Now Spreading Rapidly in US," *New York Times*, last revised February 9, 2021, www.nytimes.com/2021/02/07/health/coronavirus-variant-us-spread.html.

you were on track to reach? In other words, were you chasing a big goal, playing it safe, or simply focusing on getting things done?

When an industry or company is in motion, it's either going forward or going backward. Your career is the same way. You're either creating momentum through deeds and contributions to your company, or you're jumping from job to job and stuck making lateral moves. Look closely at your past actions. If change is needed, awareness of that fact is half the battle.

You Are Here

Now that you have everything you need to place your "I Am Here" pin on the map, let's look at a blank navigation chart with fresh eyes.

Sample Navigation Chart

	Priorities	
1.	Stabilize	
2.	Preserve	
3.	Recover	
4.	Return to Growth	

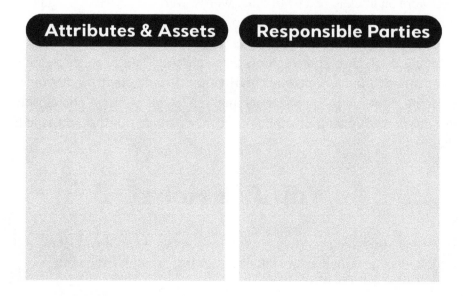

Let's officially record your waypoint now. Start by delineating your priorities, attributes and assets, and responsible parties. The people who make up your organization are what matters most, so start there. While mission and expansion might be your inspiration, place them lower on your navigation chart in a disruption. They won't lead you out of the fog. They won't respond to thousands of disrupted customers. And they won't keep your teams employed.

I'm not trying to take your vision away, but it's not important right now. The navigation chart tells you what is. Now that you know your waypoint, you can look forward to finding your way out of the fog.

As I worked with my clients over the initial months of the COVID-19 disruption, we were able to get things under relative control, even with the continued ban on cruise ships operating in North America. At the time of this book's publication, we see daylight emerging. The company has done all the right things and avoided all the wrong ones. They may not have any cruises operating yet, but they are actively pursuing other opportunities to restart the revenue generation machine and retool for the future. An impressive example of this approach is MGM, the Las Vegas resort and casino giant. They have accelerated a push into online and virtual gaming as a way to maintain the profits of gambling even when guests aren't traveling to Las Vegas and staying in their hotels, freeing themselves and their customers from a place-based relationship and opening up new revenue streams in the midst of massive disruption.

I was recently asked to help a cruise company with the reboot of the go-to-market activities after the debilitating months-long COVID pause. We laid out a plan that ultimately led to millions in new reservations for 2021 and 2022. Since the virus is still ongoing, we changed strategy to give customers confidence and permission to dream up long-term goals for cruise trips further in the future and flexible new policies to acknowledge the unknown future. That gives them something to look forward to, and it gives the cruise industry something to keep them afloat. This gives companies a fighting chance. Even though the marketplace has been still for months, it was possible to find a common point in the future when it is possible to reengage with customers and redefine the future of the company. Courage, endurance, and determination pay.

In the cruise industry and in life, there are many unknowns. No matter what disruption you face, you always have options. But you must be willing to assess where you are before you try any of them. To do the right thing at the wrong time and place is to do the wrong thing. Think long-term even if you're stunned. The fog will lift one day. Until then, "Bail, steer, repair, repeat!" All hands on deck to keep your ship safe. That requires an honest assessment of reality. Only when you're truthful about the state of things can you choose the best way to respond.

CHAPTER 3

Stay Afloat

The Second Protocol for Survival, Stability, and Success

He who has conquered doubt and fear has conquered failure.

—James Lane Allen

Nobody gets into the cruise industry for quick and easy profits. A major cruise ship can cost over $1 billion and take two years to build. The return on investment is a long-term proposition, with many risks involved.

In the worldwide cruise business, operating 24-7 on the world's oceans and rivers, visiting all seven continents, I learned one thing is certain. Disruption will happen over and over again, like the ebb and flow of the tides. It is not a question of "if"; rather, it is a question of "when," "where," and "how bad." Count on it. Prepare for it. Learn from it. Apply hard-earned lessons from disruptions past. Continuously mitigate known risks.

In the executive and advisory roles I've held over the years, I've been directly involved in several new ship projects, from concept to christening events, deployment planning, and market introduction. Also international market entry, annual revenue plans of over $1 billion, and competitive repositioning strategies costing hundreds of millions of dollars, plus mergers and acquisitions, due diligence, and post-acquisition integrations, to name a few. I advise companies on growth strategies, product development/design, technology tools, performance improvement, business recovery, marketing, distribution, pricing, data analysis and modeling, and raising capital. I evaluate and invest in start-up companies with promising technologies.

It is very challenging to earn consistent profits in the cruise business until a company reaches a certain level of scale and revenue. Once beyond that challenging break-even point, the profits and cash flow can be remarkable. The few publicly traded multibillion-dollar cruise groups that dominate the industry demonstrate the challenges and the rewards. By comparison, the smaller specialized cruise company that my family built carried operating margins and cash requirements that would send entrepreneurs in other industries spiraling into panic. Add to those slim margins the ever-present need to book tens of thousands of customers and survive economic cycles we have no control over, and it can be a brutal business. That is the very reason the cruise business has many valuable lessons for us all. Learn how to stay afloat and adapt in the cruise industry, and you can safely navigate any job, career, or business through anything.

When times are great, the objective is to operate as profitably as possible while also improving and growing the business. Consumers spend on bucket-list travel experiences, and cruise and travel companies are eager to fulfill those dreams. But when the public pulls back spending on vacations, revenue falls as well. And if we don't adjust immediately to a decrease in spending behavior, we find ourselves in trouble. In the cruise business, the true impact of a pullback in spending appears months into the future because of consumers' advance vacation-planning horizons. We can be operating at full capacity and top pricing today but have a completely different reality unfolding just a few short months ahead. It is critical to watch for such changes and make immediate adjustments before the gap between revenues and operating expenses plus overhead grows too wide, affecting profitable operations and cash flow. From an accounting perspective, looking ahead at the impact, the same math doesn't make sense anymore. And we need to make it make sense.

Every financial decision a cruise company makes affects what it is and is not able to do years into the future. And that is a conservative understatement. The reverse is also true—plans made for the future require specific activities now, milestones to meet, if they are ever to come to pass. For example, in early 2021, Seatrade Cruise News reported over $10.4 billion worth of new investments, including twenty-seven new oceangoing cruise ships, all making their maiden voyages within the calendar year.[7] These are on top of all existing cruise ships, by the way.

All the ships need passengers, the loans need to be paid, and the ships eventually need to set sail . . . all amid the pandemic pandemonium. Restart is essential, Thus, the way to figure out how to do that given the restrictions is essential.

As you know, I've both managed and advised cruise lines through uncharted economic times. Those experiences taught me the delicate balance between the necessary drive for profit and the ability to make it through tough times, despite the high cost. We'd pay almost any price to make it out in one piece, of course. That has certainly been the case during COVID-19. It's here where we develop new levels of resilience and create the stability required to weather the next storm.

The most recent notable downturn before the COVID-19 shutdown was the great recession of 2007 and 2008. I saw some companies continue to prioritize growth and maximum profits above all else and others prioritize continuity of operations and survival. Those with access to cash and a steady hand on expense control were able to make it through

---

7   Anne Kalosh, "$10bn in New Ships, 39,000 Lower Berths to Join Global Cruise Fleet in 2021," Seatrade Cruise News, January 4, 2021, www.seatrade-cruise.com/shipbuilding-refurb-equipment/10bn-new-ships-39000-lower-berths-join-global-cruise-fleet-2021.

very challenging market conditions. Not just assets—that wasn't enough. Money on paper isn't necessarily money you can spend. Even cruise companies that were worth billions had to "get liquid" and find cash to cover expenses when revenue decreased substantially, especially those companies on an aggressive growth curve with recent new ship deliveries and more on the way. The long-term economic pullback stopped a significant amount of customers from buying nice-to-have experiences like vacations of all types.

In early 2007, the cruising outlook was all sunny skies. The worst of the ripple effects of 9/11, SARS-1, and the second Iraq War had been dealt with; the economy had come back strong; cruise bookings and profits were setting new records. We'd found ways to cope with the change and prosper as a result. Safety protocols for terror attack prevention and viral outbreak mitigation brought some delays and frustration, but now they felt like the new normal. We looked toward the end of the decade with rational optimism.

That year, I, too, was ready to sail full speed ahead. A publicly traded company had brought me aboard as an executive to steer their effort to acquire and combine smaller specialty cruise companies into one portfolio. In one case, the company was able to acquire an iconic, well-known cruise brand at a high price, but one that at the time seemed reasonable, given market conditions and the performance history of that company. The seller, a much larger company, offered attractive financing terms to support their price and help cushion any future risks the new buyer might encounter. It was a very reasonable transaction, providing tens of millions of dollars in financing on attractive terms.

If you convince a larger company to sell a well-performing division to you at a reasonable price and provide you with financing terms for a large portion of the purchase price, seriously consider acting on it. The company followed my advice, accepted the deal, and completed the acquisition. Just a few short months later, I was advised by the CEO that the company had decided to pay off the entire loan early.

"Why?" I asked.

"Why not? We have the cash."

"Yes, but this is a cyclical industry, and unexpected things happen in this business. Keeping cruise ships operating when good times turn bad is expensive."

I reminded this CEO that in this business, it's unwise to give up your cash reserves unless you absolutely have to. Keep your money, I advised. Pay off the loan on schedule. No sooner.

However, the perspective of the CEO and finance team was that the large loan and interest payments associated with it were a drag on earnings per share.

Their minds were made up. I had no advance knowledge about the impending housing market collapse and its spillover effect on travel. I simply know the industry, its history of disruption, and the requirement for a high amount of liquidity.

Shortly after, I left the company. Then came the storms of the great recession, which eventually overtook the industry. The company, it turned out, did not have the cash needed to operate their way out of it. Within a year, they fired the CEO and sold several assets, including that great acquisition, through a bankruptcy proceeding. I even explored, along with others, raising capital to buy some of those assets and companies. The cruise line exists to this day under new ownership, but whenever I see their name, I feel a tinge of sadness. Overoptimism and the shortsighted pursuit of profit or stock valuation can lead to an unhealthy bravado that shoves aside the practical requirement of maintaining liquidity, not just for the good times, but especially in preparation for the inevitable downturns. The situation was avoidable, yet the outcome was inevitable. What a difference a bird in the hand—in this case, a substantial long-term loan—can make.

When sailing is smooth, it's easy to assume fair weather will continue. You feel like you can do no wrong. It feels almost imprudent to presume this pleasant status quo will change. Nonetheless, experience teaches us that those who prepare for disruption—or who are willing and able to adapt quickly—are most likely to make it through.

During the great recession, revenue projections sank. Prospects we'd counted on converting into customers lost their jobs, their homes, and even their life savings. For many, higher-cost vacation travel was much lower on the list of justifiable expenditures. Within six months, it looked like the effects of the economic slowdown were permanent. Cruise company stocks fell over 50 percent and took eight years to recover.

This was a slow leak disruption, so we at least had time to prepare for impact. We could calculate it. We might be wrong about how deep and how long it would be, but we could start responding to it. During any economic slowdown, you don't see much impact on cruises in the first four to six months. Those guests have already paid for their trips; the decision is made; the money is spent. In a terrorist attack, pandemic, or other sudden event, shock is immediate, and trips are canceled, either by the customer or the cruise line. This wasn't a disruption that prevented people from wanting to travel; it shrank the market of people who could afford to.

During the period of the great recession and for several years of its lingering impact, I helped investors and cruise-line owners see not only their way through but also new opportunities emerging as a result. Again, access to capital was a crucial factor in all cases.

The very first response to a downturn in circumstances is to reduce or delay cash expenditure. That was obvious but not easy. It never is when people's livelihoods and years of valuable skills and contributions to the company are at stake. Or when essential investments in product upgrades, new products, and more efficient technologies are underway. We also had to decide if pricing changes would work, either discounting or raising—no matter which, they are always tricky. Reducing price enough to overcome reduced demand only pays off if you have related sources of income that can still generate additional margin. For example, the giant cruise ships can sell cruise vacations at cost and still make profits from additional onboard income such as bars, casinos, spas, shops, and shore excursions. But be careful—lowering prices in other situations, such as a smaller luxury cruise line that includes all those extras in the price, usually doesn't pay off because expenses are fixed, and with less sales volume, you could face a loss. Also, it can take years to recover your pricing and the value perception of your services or product if you cut too deep. Better to balance a combination of cost cutting, selective price reduction, reducing capacity to protect price, and changing your strategy across a variety of markets and channels. Don't deal yourself a death blow with an ill-considered response to changing market conditions. Keep your eye on the prize of the inevitable return to better times and the opportunity that lies ahead.

One company in this position was a long-established Norway-based cruise line I worked with as a client from 2010 through 2016. Their primary market was extensive cruising of the Norway coastline, plus expedition cruising featuring the Arctic during summer months and Antarctica in the winter months. Truly world-class experiences for adventurous travelers. They received up to 35 percent of their business from the North American market, depending on the product. The great recession decimated their business, including US customers pulling back on discretionary spending. Their already-slim margins couldn't absorb the major revenue decline. The company pulled back their offices, staff, and marketing in North America, and it hurt them even worse. They didn't know how to regain their prior position in the market. We worked shoulder to shoulder with them on a risky, primarily results-based compensation formula to rebuild their business. Every aspect of the business came under review, including brand and product positioning, pricing and policies, vessel deployments, marketing, and distribution. No more expensive headquarters offices and multilayered expensive management staff. Past feel-good advertising and public relations efforts were replaced with hard-hitting, highly targeted database marketing programs. A shared-cost approach to marketing talent, the sales team, and the reservations center provided great cost efficiency in the rebuild phase. Within twenty-four months, North American revenues returned to prerecession levels, at a much more profitable level given the expense reductions. The company attracted the attention of a large private equity company that took it private, invested hundreds of millions of dollars in new ships, and funded a new direction for the company. We were a part of that strategic effort and helped them build North American revenues to even higher levels as their other global markets also grew. It was a hugely successful outcome, driven by necessity, innovation, risk-taking, and a passionate belief in the company and product. Today, that client is considered a global leader in sustainable adventure cruising.

It took time, but these innovative solutions together kept the company afloat long enough to outlast the great recession and its ripple effects in subsequent years. We found the approach they needed to generate revenues, reduce costs, and grow in new ways while other cruise and travel companies didn't.

What Is Keeping Your Head Above Water Worth to You?

If you walk into any big box store that sells water recreation equipment, you'll see a selection of life jackets for pleasure boating, sailing, jet skiing, kayaking, paddle boarding and canoeing. Prices range from $15 to $150, including commercial life jackets with sewn-on reflective strips. If you were shopping for essential safety gear for a day at the beach or an afternoon out on a boat, how much would you pay for a life jacket? You would probably want the best overall value based on price, quality, and function. Even if you could afford the highest price, most likely the total value equation would be your deciding factor. Nobody likes to pay more than necessary.

Now imagine you're treading frigid water beside a capsized boat. Salt water burns your nose and throat. You can't catch your breath. And you have no life jacket.

How much would you pay for one in that situation? Most people would probably trade everything they owned—house, investments, life savings, all of it—even for the one that retailed for $15.

This extreme example offers insight into the seriousness and imperative of the second protocol, stay afloat. If survivability is slipping away from your business, your career, your finances, your *anything*, you do whatever you must. Take offers and accept help that you never would have under normal circumstances. How much is making it through and regaining the future worth? That's really the question.

Surviving disruption looks much different from normal operations. You don't have the luxury of picking out the life jacket that offers the best value. When you're in protection mode, you'll often change your calculation: that is, make new choices to achieve incremental improvements to buy time to open up more options. Save the ship at all costs. As I wrote in the poem "The Ship of My Soul," bail, steer, repair, repeat.

Eight Tips to Stay Afloat

During the great recession, COVID-19, and other disruptions from terror attacks to natural disasters, I've implemented and recommended the same best practices to both organizations and individuals for how to stay afloat. When life is uncertain, finding and generating resources to last the duration are the closest thing to security there is. Here's how I, my companies, and many of my clients have kept their heads above water long enough to reach safety.

1. Reduce Expenses Quickly

Every company or individual has a combination of fixed overhead expenses and discretionary spending. Take time to consider all your expenses to see what can be reduced or eliminated. I'm not suggesting you furlough your best employees or sell all your assets. That's a last resort. Instead, can you shift your best employees to the higher cash-generating and saving activities? Can they defer some of their compensation for a period in order to help out? Or work remotely and eliminate all travel and related expenses?

Most individuals, like companies, have fixed expenses to cover. These likely include a mortgage, property taxes, insurance, utilities, medical bills, and maybe a car payment or tuition for their kids. Your core overhead is not easy to cut back on. Then there is lifestyle spending, which is easier to reduce. These are things like vacations, luxuries, and things that aren't necessities and can be deferred. In order to preserve cash, you have to move quickly on making decisions about what can be reduced. The easiest dollar you'll ever earn is the one you don't spend, especially in a period of uncertainty.

If you get stuck in denial and believe that everything will bounce back eventually without you needing to lift a finger, you're going to spend money you shouldn't, and you won't get it back. Take a really clear-eyed, hard look at what is essential and what is not, both personally and professionally. Then determine how much of the nonessential can be deferred or eliminated. Manage your expenses to keep all the money you can. Which brings us to number two.

2. Preserve Cash You Still Have

This may seem obvious at this point, but I'll say it again. Avoid paying off debts or loans early. There is a tendency to panic about debt at the wrong time. There's little to no advantage in paying off debts unnecessarily during a setback. The interest you pay is a miniscule price for the flexibility and security that cash provides. Of course, replace higher-interest debt with lower-interest debt if you can, in order to decrease interest expenses. Chances are you're going to be in the hole when this disruption is all said and done, and that's OK. The last thing you need to do is pay off debt during difficult times and economic disruptions. Do not unnecessarily reduce your cash reserves. Leave that debt right where it is. Don't be the CEO who lost the company by rapidly decreasing debt in an effort to improve earnings per share and stock valuation. Also, avoid unnecessary purchases, like new equipment, unless the ROI is immediately positive.

3. Overestimate How Much Cash You'll Need

Any disruption is like an iceberg. Typically, 90 percent of it is below the water, so, of course, you don't see that coming. You see only what's above the surface, so you don't realize how much danger is unseen.

If your business or career runs into disaster, don't underestimate how much money you'll need to get through it. In fact, conservatively over-estimate. Always assume that the disruption will last longer and be more expensive than it currently appears. That way, when you experience an unexpected problem, like a health crisis, a change in living arrange-ments, the loss of a big client, or whatever else comes along, you'll be prepared.

When the coronavirus crisis hit, what did Carnival, Royal Carib-bean, Norwegian Caribbean, and the other major cruise lines do? They immediately went looking for additional cash, even under unattractive terms. They pulled in billions and billions of dollars in cash because they did not know how long the pause would be. They needed to reassure investors they were doing what it took to increase the odds of survival. Now, even though the disruption is ongoing, they're raising and secur-ing capital, laying off some employees, keeping others, updating guests, delaying payables, and deferring expenses. All these are part of the strategy they've built to keep as much cash as possible so they can stay afloat over the long term. This requires a delicate balance of communi-cating with stakeholders and preparing potential scenarios for restart.

The mantra for a lot of these companies is to stay afloat now and be in a position to take confident actions once the path of recovery becomes clear.

4. Leverage Disruption to Get Ahead

Keeping your head above water is your primary goal, but it's not your only one. Look ahead at what your competition is planning and what new needs your target market might have. Position yourself now to take advantage of promising new opportunities.

For companies with cash on hand or access to long-term, low-in-terest loans, the great recession was a once-in-a-decade opportunity to outpace the competition. Whenever a big market gets smaller, you need a larger piece of the pie. Any competitors who survive disruption will be playing a new game, and you need to be up to their challenge. I helped companies with resources secure a disproportionate market share. That often meant accepting a lower profit margin in the short term.

For example, one strategy we employed was offering better incentives through travel agencies. We offered travel agents a bonus commission on every cruise booking for a short period as a win-win solution to help our partners and ourselves. We sharpened our competitive stance with selective offer-match programs, and we strengthened our past-guest loyalty benefits to ensure their next trip was with us. We would not concede one precious dollar of revenue to a competitor. We also opened new distribution channels, including new and expanded online promotions, and entered international markets such as the UK, Australia, and New Zealand. Anything and everything to keep the faucet of new business open. Across our larger corporation of multiple cruise lines, we instituted a cross-marketing and lead-sharing initiative, which collectively saved us millions of dollars in advertising and provided ready access to known cruise buyers, especially for the smaller brands in our group.

Another method I used in downturns was to shift higher percentages of capacity into more affordable destinations and itineraries. When the market is strong and people are rewarding themselves with bucket-list experiences, we want to push capacity into places where the most money can be made. But when there's an economic disruption and people are spending less, you want to fill as much capacity as possible. One of the best ways to do that is to align that capacity with a new demand pattern. The fortunate thing in the cruise industry is that we have these mobile assets. I don't mean to make it sound easy. It takes time. However, because of the nature of our business, we can move ships from expensive destinations that require long flights and extra hotel stays to less expensive ones in order to reach destinations closer to home. Just look at the way the cruise industry has developed home ports along every stretch of North American coastline in order to provide convenient, close-to-home cruise vacations to the Caribbean, Mexico, Canada, and Alaska, right on the doorstep of tens of millions of potential customers. That comes in handy during a downturn when more ships must shift from Europe, South America, and Asia cruises to the more affordable destinations.

If the overall trip is less expensive and there are fewer operating costs for the ships in those areas, you can charge a lower price point and broaden your market. All of a sudden, you open that aperture of destinations and price points, and you've just increased your ability to capture a disproportionate share of whatever market exists.

5. Create Multiple Sources of Income

When you face disruption, multiple streams of income or new income sources may be necessary to get you back to where you were. Even if you don't need the additional income today, don't dig the hole deeper than it has to be; don't continue into the unknown with insufficient resources.

Creating additional revenue sources also has the benefit of making you more prepared for the next inevitable disruption. As you generate these new sources of income (whether that's taking on additional clients, expanding your business to a different market or product, starting your own small business on the side, or even getting a part-time job on the weekends), you learn how to rate and manage multiple revenue streams. Developing this skill gives you a more confident mindset that makes you practically watertight and more able to adjust to unexpected events.

Bottom line: having multiple sources of income makes you resilient under any circumstances. There are so many people who don't have the first clue how to make a dollar outside their primary salaried or hourly income. But there's good news. If you can make that first dollar, you can learn to make ten times, then a hundred times, then a thousand times that. While this isn't a book about starting side hustles or developing new products, there are plenty of resources available if you need them. For individuals, I would recommend the book *Side Hustle: From Idea to Income in 27 Days* by Chris Guillebeau. For business owners, I recommend *The Sticking Point Solution: 9 Ways to Move Your Business from Stagnation to Stunning Growth in Tough Economic Times* by Jay Abraham. And any other avenue that helps you multiply your streams of cash will be beneficial.

If you're in a tight financial spot and don't have the time to create a new income stream, a small loan is an option. I've advised many companies to look into loans over the years. Arranging a line of credit or a loan before you need it and while you are bankable is critical. You'll often pay nothing to have those funds at the ready, only incurring interest and payments when and if you begin to use them. Debt has two sides. It can be beneficial or detrimental, depending on the way you use it. The best debt in the world is that which keeps you afloat on stormy seas, assuming you have the fortitude and vision to recover after the event. While payments on the loan will come due in the future, for the time being, that capital infusion may just save your business and livelihood.

If a crisis looks to go on longer than initially expected, accept more financing. As we saw in the examples during the great recession, if you have positioned yourself in a place where you can get liquid, you can reach informed assumptions in a calm manner. When you're pushing the envelope like the CEO who was eager to push up the company profits without considering the liquidity ramifications, you're not positioned well, and you may lose everything.

6. Protect Your Existing Income

As you're expanding your sources of revenue, you want to be aware if any source of income is at risk, especially over the long term. Consider how confident you are in your current situation. Your primary source of income might be reduced at the moment if the company you work for or the clients you're serving are suffering. Evaluate your sources of income not just for the immediate impact but for the longer term.

Start thinking about whether you need to replace some or all of your revenue and how soon, whether you're getting income from your own business, through contracting and consulting, or from several sources. Distinguish between the sources that are likely to endure and those that will get worse and possibly go away. I found myself working with a lot of clients on this issue. I'm a long-term value thinker, and I have long relationships with clients. I'm not going to leave someone in a pinch just because they can't pay me right away. I'm not going to give less value. I help them through the problem so that they *can* pay their expenses and obligations.

Don't completely dismiss the sources of income that are not as profitable as they were in the past at the moment. Instead, look at the whole playing field and determine what's coming from where. Cash is cash. For each source of income, decide if you are going to see it through or make a change. You need to be playing the long game. I've seen client companies have a knee-jerk reaction and stop all marketing spending when, in fact, the right spending could produce even more cash. The old rule may have been "We require a fifteen-times return on each marketing dollar spent." The new rule, in disruption: "We'll take a four-times return on each marketing dollar spent."

7. Push Promising Projects into the Future

If unexpected trouble emerges when you're in the midst of exciting plans, push them further into the future. Don't dismiss or cancel them; just temporarily relieve yourself of the burden of self-imposed deadlines. Shift your definition of success on your projects. Instead of finishing a particular product this quarter, commit to having it ready to go two years from now. Be strategic, always aware of the precious yet perishable resource: cash.

In times of ultra-lean cruise operations, we've pushed future events even further out into the future, delaying new ship construction contracts and even delaying delivery of new ships currently under construction. You have time to make changes when you push things further out than you might have preferred. It's still the same company with the same plan, just a different time line with higher odds of success. If cruise lines had stuck with their original five-year plans during the great recession, their odds of achieving them would have been zero. By thinking differently and pushing plans a little further out, we could stay on course to achieve a recovery. The truth is that we're all in this for the long run, regardless of whether it is a cruise line, a business in another industry, or your career. Take comfort in that long-view commitment and give yourself permission to change the time line for your objectives and strategies when conditions turn against you. You may not progress at the same speed, but disruption is not a race. Surviving and then continuing on is winning.

Decades of investment, innovation, and growth are at stake during a disruption. The global extended pause brought about by the pandemic pushed the cruise industry to the proverbial edge of possible extinction. Think of the incredible work required to design and build world-class experiences in the travel industry. Then the additional effort and investment to make them viable and successful in the marketplace with brand positioning, marketing, communications, distribution, sales, reservations, inventory, and yield management. And most importantly, the decades of developing a workforce of hundreds of thousands of skilled, committed men and women worldwide, who are the ones who actually make the cruise industry so successful. Most of whom lost their jobs, which may not return to the cruise industry for years, if ever. All this work and these resources are generating annual revenue of roughly $45 billion. When COVID-19 brought cruising to a full stop, cruise lines had to refund much of that revenue or convince customers to take a more valuable credit for use on a future cruise instead of a refund. But they couldn't get refunds for the money spent building the industry. The fleets of ships were built, with more coming. The marketing campaigns had run. The salaries were paid. The global headquarters, technology centers, and training facilities had been put in place. The revenue was gone, but these expenses remained and could not be recouped. The cruise companies had to raise billions of dollars in cash to cover expenses, past, present, and future. They sold stock and borrowed money at what would normally be considered unacceptable terms and interest rates. These new costs of capital have to be amortized and capitalized against future profits. Some assets, like older ships, were sold to raise cash, at prices requiring write-offs against the balance sheet. Cruise companies went without revenue for the longest period in industry history. Those that survived focused on one priority: stay liquid and capable of taking proactive measures toward recovery. As long as they remain viable, they can rebuild and reclaim the promise of the future. Run out of cash, and it's over.

When your primary focus is conserving cash, don't devote resources to a project that won't produce a relatively quick payback in terms of cash flow. That's a sure way to end up having to take more drastic measures later, such as laying off your most valuable employees. A new project that gets new revenue coming in next month? Go for it. A plan that sees an increase in profits over the next five years? First make sure you can go the distance for five years to benefit from it.

Financial readiness is an ongoing process, and a lot of the planning happens before a disruption is in play. With proper planning, you can take steps to increase liquidity and cash flow at the first sign of a financially risky situation. That's how you fall asleep on otherwise sleepless nights. You can protect cash flow by shedding expenses to a degree, but to stay ahead requires cash reserves and ready sources of additional cash, such as a line of credit.

8. Close the Anxiety Gap

I believe that situational anxiety, different from medical anxiety, represents a gap between what we say or tell ourselves and others and what we actually do. Actions don't lie or compromise. They are absolute. The anxiety comes from the incongruence between how we want to interpret or perceive things and how they actually are.

I call that the anxiety gap. All situational anxiety resides within that gap. The anxiety gap can be quantified per issue and summed up in total for all issues where there are such gaps. Then a strategy to reduce that anxiety, issue by issue, gap by gap, can be identified, undertaken, measured, and adjusted.

Here's a simple gap example: "I'm overweight. I don't feel good. My clothes don't fit. I need to lose ten pounds. I'm going to start a diet" versus "I weigh 180 pounds. I've weighed this for months. It's more than I weighed last year. I don't watch what I eat. I know my actions are sabotaging my stated goal of losing weight."

The anxiety gap formula closes that gap. In this example, the formula is obvious: ten pounds = 35,000 calories. Reducing my consumption of calories by 3,500 per week will contribute to a loss of ten pounds.

This formula is dynamic in that as change occurs in either direction, the formula changes with it. This is true in all categories—health and fitness, personal finances, career and professional relationships, energy, happiness, personal growth, and so on. You can close the anxiety gap to zero by aligning what you say with what you do. Both sides of that equation must align. When they do, issue after issue, your total anxiety reduces dramatically—eventually, all the way to nothing.

These eight tips can feel like a lot to remember when you're under financial pressure. Fortunately, we can bring them together with a versatile tool called a waterfall chart.

The Financial Insights of a Waterfall

There's "google something," and then there's "google earth something," which means the farther in you look, the smaller but clearer your view is. At any time, you can reverse directions and zoom out. You go from little detail to seeing snow-capped mountains and cities and borders and coasts.

Logging each income/revenue line item as well as expenses is like zooming in. You can see the details, but you can also get lost in the details.

So zoom out when you need to in order to see the financial lay of the land. In this case, that means adding up the income categories and subtracting expenses. What do you have left? That is your financial earth, zoomed all the way out.

The waterfall chart presented below helps you zoom in and out as needed.[8] The chart gives you a visual of where you are, what you need, and how you can incrementally get it. It shows a cascade of all your financial streams: income and expenditures, positive and negative, good and bad. Changes over time, both historic and future, projected. A waterfall chart can work for everyone, from big organizations down to self-employed solopreneurs. You can create one per month, per quarter, or per year, depending on your needs. Because it gives a much better picture of the real size and impacts of a disruption and reveals areas you might be ignoring, you can use a waterfall chart to plot your way through and out of the crisis.

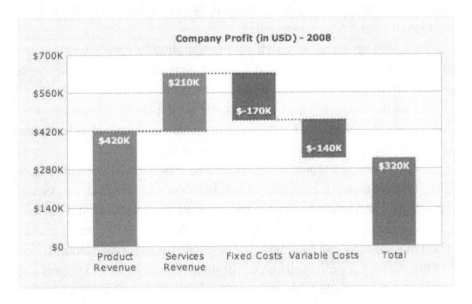

Moving left to right, start with all forms of income, whether salary, revenue, side businesses, or even loans. Each income stacks on top of the next, showing both the incremental additional amount and your total on the left side. From there, add your expenses. Fixed expenses like salaries for a business or utilities for a family are first. Variable expenses

---

8   FusionCharts Blog, https://fusioncharts.typepad.com/.a/6a010534c80b-99970c0115724aac3e970b-800wi, CC by SA 4.0, https://commons.wikimedia.org/w/index.php?curid=7591537.

come next. Then subtract your expenses from your income to get your total on the right.

As you can see, your waterfall chart with all income and expenses reveals your current situation in detail. It also helps you calculate the financial resources you'll need in the event any of your income plummets or any of your expenses skyrocket.

For simplicity, the chart above has incomes and expenses lumped together, but it may be more useful to list each revenue stream and expense type. This is especially helpful for eight-to-five wage earners and people who feel like they don't have a lot of options. That said, the simpler the better. The chart only works when you work the chart, and that means it must be easy at a glance to comprehend and communicate changes in your financial situation.

Once you create your chart, save a template to create a new chart quickly for the next month, quarter, or year. You can also lay your monthly charts side by side to analyze changes over time.

If you're doing a waterfall chart for your personal finances, start with your main source of income. Then add any type of side hustle, freelance work, or other income. Then come expenses.

If you're doing a waterfall for your business, start with income from sales, broken down into different products or services and sources, if applicable. Then move to your expenses—utilities, salaries and payroll, operating expenses, and so on. You'll be able to visualize and measure different scenarios and the impact of actions you are considering. If you do a chart every month, you can cut or delay discretionary expenses and see where you can add to your income. The waterfall chart is a tool that can help ensure that you stay afloat.

Your personal financial situation is not much different from any business or organization. We all have fixed, essential expenses like a mortgage and groceries. We also have lifestyle discretionary expenses like vacations, dining out, and entertainment. Move quickly and consider your personal expenses in much the same way you would in a business. Do not let denial and false hope make you lose precious cash that you cannot get back.

If you complete your waterfall chart and you're happy with that number on the right, good. But I would advise you to reconsider tip three—overestimate how much cash you'll need. Things could get worse. Is it possible to utilize the first tip and reduce those costs, fixed or variable? Is it worth it to essentially "buy" peace of mind in this way? I'm not suggesting obsessive expense micromanagement down to the cent or intentional wage deflation. When skies are clear, find a course that balances comfort and frugality. That will mean a lot more comfort when a storm strikes.

Another thing I appreciate about waterfall charts is the way they show a whole business at scale. They're one of the best visual tools for quickly taking overwhelming information that you're looking at on a spreadsheet and making it make sense. A waterfall chart can show what's changed or needs to change. For example, how did we miss our plan by so much? Or what impact did new sources of revenue and categories of expense have on this year's result? You can also use your waterfall chart to make future projections. If you want to go from a $20 million profit this year to $25 million next year, you can spot at a glance how to drive that growth. You start with your $20 million on one end and your $25 million on the other. In between, you build little steps that close the gap. One initiative delivers $1 million of that growth. Perhaps the next one gives you $250,000. Then you seize an opportunity that gives you $2 million and so on.

Without the waterfall chart, you can be left wondering how you missed your budget. With the chart, you can see very clearly where you began, where you ended up, and where you did better or worse than planned. The steps between the two are simple to understand for everyone involved. It's also a quick way to communicate to others what's going on. The changes that occurred can be broken up into multiple categories for easy analysis.

Remember the Norway cruise company that I helped stay afloat through the great recession? They used a waterfall chart during 2007 and 2008. They made all the decisions they had to in order to stay afloat financially. And they did. The company survived the recession and outlasted their competitors because they prioritized cash flow first and foremost. The same advice applies to all organizations and individuals: the more positive cash flow you can create and the more cash reserves you have on hand to spend or invest as needed, the more options you have. This company survives to this day because they're continuously willing to creatively adapt and find solutions that are outside the box.

If you want to stay afloat, keep all the cash and access to liquidity you can on hand and do whatever it takes to get whatever you need for the disruption's duration. Put as much space between yourself and an unrecoverable situation as possible. That way, you'll be in the best position to direct and restart your journey when conditions allow.

CHAPTER 4

Find Your First First

The Third Protocol for Survival, Stability, and Success

A strong soul shines after every storm.

—Unknown

O n November 1st, 2020, everything changed. Again. An entire industry that was thrown into a reverse thrust and full stop months earlier was suddenly told to prepare to restart its engine. This was after the summer of no cruises—no ships transporting guests to Alaska or along Canada's scenic waterways, the coastal cities of Europe and the Mediterranean, or even the pure-blue Caribbean for seven months straight. The last time our industry went a summer without a ship on the water prior to COVID-19 was the day before history's first cruise ship set sail, *Prinzessin Victoria Luise*, a German passenger cruise liner that launched on June 29, 1900.

One doesn't simply bring 120 years' worth of momentum to a halt and then expect it all to restart seamlessly. The Centers for Disease Control's no-sail order had been extended month by month through October 31. The pandemic itself and the authorities' attempts to "flatten the curve" by any means necessary left cruise industry leaders uncertain as to how to plan for fall and winter cruises—if at all. Would the CDC continue to extend the moratorium on passenger cruises? Would the COVID pandemic abate?

As October 31 neared, the opposite happened. In the early days of fall 2020, the CDC and other regulatory bodies held meetings to discuss the requirements for a safe cruise industry restart. A "healthy sail panel" made up of health-care professionals, disease specialists, and cruise line representatives came up with a list of seventy-four recommendations to make cruise ships safe enough to start sailing again, under the assumption that this new virus, like the flu, was one we would all have to learn to live and operate our businesses with.[9] The result of these recommendations led to a report certified by the CDC outlining a restart of the cruise industry by passing through multiple rigid phases.

As you might expect with any government agency putting out a set of conditions for an industry, there were complications. "Prepare to start your engines" is very different from "Start your engines." Some recommendations made sense, such as boosting air circulation within ships and adopting additional sanitization practices. But others were unclear or unrealistic—or both. For example, one of the seventy-four recommendations was that no cruise could be longer than seven days. The average cruise runs seven days, but many last two weeks or longer. An around-the-world cruise is more than a hundred days long. Most European cruises are ten to fourteen days long. Why would the cleaning protocols that apply to seven-day cruises not work for fourteen- or twenty-one-day cruises? The CDC-certified protocols also included an insistence that cruise lines add a warning to all marketing materials that

---

9   Shannon McMahon, "Cruises Can Begin Phased Return Starting Nov. 1 Under New Protocols, CDC Says," *Washington Post*, October 30, 2020, www.washington-post.com/travel/2020/10/30/cruise-covid-ban-lifted/.

any cruise could be canceled or changed at any moment, with potential quarantine. This meant that all marketing communications already printed or published had to be redesigned and reprinted. And prospective cruise customers would be given stern and negative warnings when making a buying decision.

These and other crippling expectations slowed every cruise company from wanting to restart. It wasn't the CDC's fault. Neither they nor any other regulators wanted the restart to be intentionally difficult. But when the seventy-four safe restart recommendations made it into the hands of cruise operators, there was a lot to digest and attempt to clarify. How did all this fit within a company's existing practices in the areas of health, safety, and satisfaction of guests? And the same commitment to the health and safety of team members, the ports visited, and the communities we operate in? Despite the encouraging restart development, the industry had to determine how best to operationalize all these new requirements and communicate the new rules in a way that was consistent with its promise to guests and duty of care to employees.

Easier said than done. There were other considerations beyond regulation compliance and operational excellence. For example, how would a travel agent be knowledgeable enough about the particular practices of each cruise company to accurately answer the questions of potential guests? How could these new safety procedures be incorporated into an already challenging operational environment, without fail, in order to keep both guests and crew safe? And how to do it in ways that still allowed guests to relax and enjoy themselves and not feel constrained by the requirements or that they were spending time in a medical clinic rather than escaping to the freedom of the seas?

We had to reengage the marketplace before a single ship could leave port. The focus shifted from "safe return to port" to "safe to sail from port." Cruise companies had to restart business operations months before they launched the first cruise. Before any cruises could be operated, no matter the regulatory conditions, we had to find out where and when customers were willing to book.

Despite the uncertainty, the industry felt a collective wave of relief when the no-sail order expired, as did avid cruise travelers, and the new conditional sail order came into effect on November 1:

> The initial phases of the latest order will require ship operators to demonstrate adherence to testing, quarantine, isolation and social distancing requirements to protect crew on board while building the necessary laboratory capacity to test staff and eventual passengers.[10]

The CDC required that cruise lines run simulated cruises to ensure their ships could follow the new health and safety protocols. Operating a series of test cruises at great expense without a single paying guest on board meant extraordinary additional investment with no immediate return.

The major North America cruise companies, wanting to restore operations sooner than later, began preparations in accordance with the CDC regulations. All announced projected start-up dates in the late spring or early summer of 2021 to allow time not only to comply with CDC regulations but also to determine what effect the newly approved vaccines might have on near-term business operations. Perhaps the success of the vaccines would reduce the need for such stringent operating conditions. At least a time line was becoming more clear. Finally, we saw what looked to be the outer edge of the fog. We might not be on the other side of the storm, but at least we were in a different place from where we'd spent the past six months.

Some cruise lines operating outside North America, in Asia and Europe, pushed the restart envelope more aggressively. A France-based cruise line that I've done business with in the past was the very first cruise back. After receiving government approval, they launched several ships at once. There were enough guests itching to be back on the water that little marketing was needed to fill their first itineraries, and

---

10   Kaelan Deese, "CDC to Lift 'No Sail' Order Allowing 'Simulation' Cruises," The Hill, October 30, 2020, https://thehill.com/policy/transportation/ports-waterways/523678-cdc-to-lift-no-sail-order-allowing-simulation-cruises.

ships were in action beginning in mid-July 2020. Unfortunately, the company experienced two notable COVID outbreaks that required the interruption of cruises underway and sent one ship into quarantine and all the others back to port with future cruises canceled. Suddenly, a company with a promising restart canceled everything—no future sailings on the horizon. This was seen as a major setback for the entire industry. Two Norway-based cruise operators also tried and failed to restart operations as a result of onboard COVID outbreaks that required quarantines and cancellation of future planned sailings.

North American cruise operators learned from those early unsuccessful attempts. There's a lot to get right, and the cost of getting it wrong is severe. I regularly reminded my clients of the first thing they should prioritize as they restarted. I call this the "first first."

While much hope was being pinned on the cruise industry's first first of developing and implementing a complex set of protocols and convincing cruise customers to adhere to them, there were several examples from those early restart attempts that suggested there may be no set of operating procedures that would be 100 percent successful at preventing COVID cases from getting through the cruise-line defenses. Thus, a new and, in my opinion, the only realistic first first began to emerge: the vaccines and widespread inoculations.

As the time line for approval and distribution of the new COVID-19 vaccines began to overlap the cruise industry's preparations to implement the new CDC protocols and requirements, the realization that a vaccine, and not just protocols, would be necessary to save the cruise industry started to sink in. The effectiveness, speed, and potentially widespread administration of the new vaccines were potential game changers. The question across the industry became "Do we wait for the vaccines and require all crew members and guests to be vaccinated prior to coming aboard our ships?" This has been my recommendation to cruise operators since the outset. I referred to it as the "experience normal" strategy—a promise to guests that under such a policy, they could experience cruising without many of the onerous restrictions and protocols required in the absence of a vaccine bubble and with high confidence that their cruise vacation plans would not be canceled. I predict that all the major cruise operators will embrace some or all of this strategy as some airlines and even countries have already begun to require all travelers be vaccinated. It is the only viable way to ensure the health and safety of guests, crew, and communities visited and to avoid the financial, operational, and public perception setbacks of failed protocols. It is a much quicker route back to full operation for the cruise lines and restoring full confidence for their guests. The point here is that sometimes, the most obvious first first is the right one, even though it initially seems impossible to attain. When COVID sidelined the cruise industry, vaccines were a far hope on the horizon. Thus, new protocols, a tried and trusted solution from the past, became the envisioned first that would get the industry back in operation as soon as possible. But this proved not to be the case. Solutions from the past may be only part of the answer to new disruptions. Be sure that you consider a broader context when identifying your first first.

What's Your First First?

Your first first in any disruption is the one thing that, if you screw it up, means everything falls apart. You would have been better off doing nothing at all. This is equally true when coming out of the disruption.

For most people and companies, there are first firsts to determine among the risks of restart. What's going to hit you first as you proceed out of the fog? While you're working on all the big stuff, be specific about the one thing that, if lost, loses everything. It's like triage—what's the one thing you have to do to keep a person from dying? Or, in this case, your business?

Right now, the Alaska 2021 cruise season restart is a case in point. It is a complex situation with many uncertainties—the type of uncertainties that make first first decision-making and action taking very difficult. The many variables involve determining the cruise start dates and season schedule; repositioning ships from layup locations around the world to the West Coast cruise ports—Seattle, Washington, and Vancouver, British Columbia—in accordance with those start dates;

reactivating and recruiting officers and crew to man the ships; turning global supply chains back on to support the ships; conforming with CDC "return to sail" protocols and regulations, including the pre-operation test cruises and limiting all cruises to seven days' maximum length, which, in some cases, required a complete replanning of itineraries; determining when the Canadian border would open to US travelers and when US and Canadian ports would reopen to cruise ships; and implementing new marketing campaigns that accurately describe what the cruising experience will entail (testing, masks, social distancing, limited exploring ashore, the potential of quarantine and cancellation in the event of a COVID outbreak aboard ship). These are just some of the considerations. There is also the very basic consideration of whether, and under what conditions, the Alaska 2021 cruise season will be financially viable. That answer is different for each cruise line, big and small. There is definitely a financial tipping point at which decisions will be made not to position ships and not to operate any Alaska cruises.

So, in this situation, what is the first first? My experience says that the first priority is to determine that financial tipping point. What are the conditions under which operating is financially viable, and how likely are those conditions to come about? Perhaps there are no conditions under which the 2021 Alaska cruise season makes sense for some cruise lines, and therefore, they need to turn their focus quickly to alternative scenarios. Every day of not operating and not earning revenues and profits is excruciating and difficult. But at least the costs and risks of not operating are known, predictable, and manageable. Once operations commence, a whole new set of operational risks must be undertaken and overcome.

For those cruise lines that conclude that operating some or all of their original 2021 Alaska schedule is within the tipping-point calculation, their next first first will be to immediately determine whether the individual ports of call in Alaska and British Columbia around which their cruises are scheduled, as well as the Canadian border, will be open for business in time for the start of the season, typically in May. My experience has been that it is the smaller details that can undo everything. Thus, before anything else on the list, it is critical to know what the government regulatory agencies and individual ports of call in British Columbia and Alaska are able and willing to commit to in terms of accepting cruise ship visits.

The number one piece of advice I offered companies looking to get operating again in November 2020 was to consider how badly they really wanted to be a maverick. Much of the new CDC report could be considered mandatory. Other aspects of it could be considered more flexible, with testing to see how things go. If you're a maverick and you're not in the United States with the CDC's stringent oversight and regulatory restrictions, you might want to restart quickly, ahead of the competition. These other European brands were in a more flexible regulatory environment. If they wanted to risk cruises during COVID, they could, subject to sensible testing and sanitation plans. However, that didn't pay off for most. Even while following all the recommendations, they couldn't be 100 percent successful in preventing someone testing positive with the virus from somehow ending up on a ship somewhere.

Think about the fog you're in right now. What's the one thing that, if you get it wrong, will keep you in the fog longer than if you get it right? For the cruise industry, the first first for the COVID restart was not to let an outbreak happen on a ship. Avoid more ugly quarantines like those that upended the entire industry at the outset of the pandemic. The first first was *not* maximum profit from the first cruises back. If an outbreak occurred, even the most risk-averse operators would suffer the consequences. Cruise companies had to move step by step out of this mess in collaboration with the CDC and other regulatory bodies at the regional and local levels. That way, when the inevitable incident occurred, they would have the support needed to get through it.

The tentative COVID-19 restart reminded me why it's wiser to put what matters first first. It's foolish to operate as a maverick, pursuing high-risk, low-reward outcomes. In all things, choose a cooperative agenda to absorb the unexpected and react accordingly. When there is so much at stake, this can be a challenge if you're not a big company with significant resources. Smaller brands and entrepreneurs may not be as prepared or have the discipline of patience, so they're more likely to choose a maverick approach. Smaller, niche-market cruise companies have to think very carefully about what they'll do if things go wrong.

Preventing the worst-case scenario will remain the first first throughout the cruise industry restart. Keep from sinking chances for recovery simply because of moving too quickly. More uncontrolled outbreaks and they'll be worse off than if they had kept the ships laid up and simply waited longer. Never turn disruption into disaster.

Once your first first is identified, you have a way to manage your next steps. Accomplish the first first and see what happens. Are you still here? Out of the red? Safe? Then you can move on to your second first, then your third first, and so on. This prevents you from trying to do too much at once, which is human (and organizational) nature. It's easy to get ahead of yourself quickly before the crisis is resolved. If you slow down and do one thing at a time, first things first, you have a path forward no matter what you're facing.

Proceeding with Caution

Restarting anything after a disruption is never easy, especially if you're a smaller company or extremely tight on cash. One might think it should be easier to start than to stop. But the shutdown surrounding COVID was unlike anything we'd experienced before. The length and depth of it completely changed the complexities of a restart.

Restart for some means a fresh start, and, in some cases, it means a fast track to the future—depending on the trajectory and course of each company before COVID and the decisions and actions taken in the midst of the disruption. A disruption on this scale exposes all the weaknesses and strengths of your business model, brand, product, management team, employee group, and other critical stakeholders.

Rarely, if ever, do we have a choice whether or not our lives and businesses get disrupted. Disruption often brings those in its midst to an unexpected stop, either by force or out of an abundance of caution. Operating in and advising the cruise industry and collecting life experience over the last few decades have taught me that we usually have a choice in how long we remain in the fog once it begins to clear. Do the wrong thing (or the right thing too soon) in a restart, and things can go from bad to worse.

When disruption shrouds a once-clear future in uncertainty, you already know you need to slow down. Put that original financial goal on hold. Pause and retool your advertising campaign. Delay that next investment. But when the fog begins to lift, it's tempting to restart your engines and sail full speed ahead. The coast is nearly clear! Or is it?

In the same way cruise companies focused on avoiding onboard outbreaks in the latter months of 2020, your priority coming out of crisis is failure prevention, *not* revenue generation. There are a lot of things that can screw up operation, the foremost of which is restarting too soon and too fast. When cruise industry leaders began planning to get back into service, they were restarting from a full stop. The industry had collided with the jagged reality of an aggressive global outbreak, restrictive regulations to prevent its spread, and public perception that cruise ships are giant petri dishes. Start too soon, and the virus might be too prevalent for mitigation activities to have a chance. Recovery will come with patience and a cautious phased return to operations. In two to three years, past experience suggests, the industry can rebuild momentum and reach the $45 billion threshold once again, if not a higher one. And it will do so with a leaner and more disruption-protected business model.

Even so, "Hurry up and wait" is difficult advice for any leader to hear, despite the risks of restart. CEOs, business owners, and entrepreneurs have a drive to create, produce, and deliver. If you have a business, you have promises to keep and expectations to fulfill. This is why assertive visionaries in any industry at any level need the first first protocol to keep overeagerness from leading to bad decisions. The full-speed-ahead-no-matter-what mindset in the midst of a disruption can blind even seasoned executives. Optimism and an appetite for risk cloud your judgment. They hide the severity of the potential consequences of your next actions. The first first enables you to exercise restraint when you just want to be done with the waiting.

In the new disrupted environment, the unknowns must be identified, considered, and weighed individually and then collectively, like a complex puzzle of risk and opportunity. Cruise companies could not possibly relaunch a multi-ship fleet in a compressed period and complete those voyages successfully. I suggested they change their mindset from "operating at a loss" to "investing in a proof of concept." The goal was a series of safe cruises running efficiently with new protocols being perfected such that they could be replicated with confidence on additional ships and in the hands of an expanding number of employees.

Cruise leadership held open discussions with the regulators, financial markets, their employees, and the public about the restart plan. For a few cruise companies, that plan meant to continue waiting for more optimal operating conditions. Not every company had the financial capacity to hold out. Many of the CDC requirements were costly and difficult to implement. The costs of waiting were accumulating, and people were getting anxious doing nothing. Everybody was worried about raising more cash because the advance spending that restarting requires is enormous, never mind the cost of operating the ships, probably at a loss for some time. They had to rehire crew, bring the ships back out of layup status, and get them provisioned and ready. Then all the port arrangements needed to be made. There were a lot of moving parts, and they all required cash. And the first test cruises had to be operated for free, with cruise lines making open invitations to past guests and the public to sign up for a chance to cruise for free on a practice cruise applying all the required protocols. Those first voyages would certainly be major money losers, but they were a start.

Still, the math had to make sense down to the dime. Cruising is extremely expensive for operators, unlike many cottage industries. A factory can resell manufactured goods and somewhat control production volume to match fluctuations in demand. The cruise industry sells a perishable good. Like hotels and airlines, it's all about inventory and revenue management. A ship that sails with empty, unsold cabins has lost that revenue forever. When selling perishable inventory, you realize how unforgiving time is. There is a curve, a booking pace, to keep up with revenue. Fall off that curve, and you have more revenue to earn in even less time. If you're trying to fill eighteen thousand beds across fourteen ships each and every week, you have a good idea of the pace required to get it done. There are hundreds of coordinated actions to take, but you cannot lose sight of the coming collision of time and perishable inventory. Every ship, every voyage, every cabin—it is a relentless race against time to avoid an irrecoverable loss of revenue opportunity, which is the key to profitability.

But like preventing a coronavirus outbreak, not all first firsts are financial. Many are not. Consider the first first of the disruption following 9/11. When ships returned to international waters during the early days of the war on terror, the cruise industry's first first was terrorism prevention. This included implementing TSA-like security procedures, screening all guests, crew, luggage, and supplies. Prescreening passenger lists against the international no-fly lists. Coast guard security escorts into and out of ports of call and docking areas. New security perimeters on land and water surrounding the massive cruise ships because of worries that they were attractive terrorism targets. As an industry, we took all this in stride in our total commitment to ensuring the safety of our guests and crew.

Those developments may not have been the obvious right way to prepare for restart after the towers fell. The first first doesn't make an immediate appearance in most recovery plans because it's often not evident. No decision is easy in the fog, especially those that involve recovery rather than survival. For the first time since the crisis hit, you get a glimpse of the new normal. It's coming. It's clearer. If you can just . . . make it . . . out. When hope is strongest, the risks are greatest.

So how do you find your one first first?

How to Choose One First First from the Second Many

I like to work from the inside out in these situations. What is the epicenter from which your decisions and actions radiate outward in concentric rings of influence?

Financial resources buy time, and for many this is the first first of surviving disruption, but is it the first first to moving forward beyond the event? It may be a critical requirement, but, as is the case for the cruise industry with COVID-19, the essence, the very core, of recovering the business is the ability to return to safe and dependable operations. In such a case, the vaccine and new protocols to meet new regulations are the essential first firsts for restart. When you look beyond survivability, what is the first first in your recovery journey?

Here's an iterative process for answering that question. I call it "next best action." It is the one thing you can do. The only thing. Remember Aron Ralston, the rock climber who cut off his own arm? To get free, limb removal was obviously his "first first" because it was his "one and only."

A recent viral video showed passersby lifting an SUV off a run-over pedestrian in Manhattan. Not running a woman over is the ideal outcome, but in that high-stakes situation, fellow citizens did the one and only thing they could. With their bare hands, they lifted a full-size car off the ground.

Relate these life-or-death scenarios to your own. What must be done to preserve life and limit injury, if at all possible? Your next best action becomes starkly clear. Survive or die. So make the first incision. Be first to get your hands under the bumper. Take the first step. Make the first call. Find the first customer. And if you can't do any of that, ask for help.

Simply knowing that you need to identify a sole priority as you make your way out of disruption fails to tell you what that priority is. With cruising, in response to COVID, even though the first first was to complete a cruise without an onboard outbreak, they also couldn't lose all their money in the process. What good would it be if the cure was worse than the storm?

If you don't know what your first priority should be, consider the main issues affecting your restart or revamp. I prefer to step into my home office or another quiet place. No electronics on or notifications to distract me. It's only me, a journal, and a fountain pen. I think deeply about the situation and jot down everything that comes to mind that could delay recovery. What will hurt if I don't get it done? What's going to completely stop me if I get it wrong? Once I understand these issues, I enter my notes on the computer, ordering each recovery risk from absolute ruin to simple annoyances. That's how I choose where to start. From that first first, it's significantly less stressful to plan for a reset.

Make this list, find your first first, and you're ready to plan.

Four Steps to a Realistic Reset Plan

Executives, founders, and entrepreneurs who've built or run successful enduring companies use this four-step framework to plan a strategy following a disruption. These instructions offer guidance to let you plan specific to your needs.

1. Square Up

See the big picture for what it is and what it could become. Decide: "Eyes on the Prize" or "Find the Exit." Square up your objectives to what must come first. Go back to the list of firsts you wrote down and reordered. At what point in recovery does it make good business sense to transition from defense to offense, from responding to events to influencing outcomes? Your priority placement on your list of steps reflects your experience, judgment, and objectives. Look forward to those goals without looking past what has to get done first. If you cannot identify a compelling reason, a "prize" to fight for, then frankly consider whether you should be exploring all your options for completely exiting the situation and starting fresh. Sometimes carrying forward the weight of the past makes no sense.

2. Layer Priorities

Develop a range of detailed scenarios to help you uncover those key variables that define your situation and which of those variable(s) is common to launching any of those scenarios. The variable(s) common across different scenarios are the ones to focus on most.

As you act on your first step, consider how you'll incorporate your second, third, and so on. Each must build on the next while still keeping your first step . . . well, first. For example, in the aftermath of COVID, cruise lines are focused on "restart," with the first step of completing voyages with successful new protocols to prevent an occurrence of outbreak. A second step will be bringing multiple ships into service. A third step is to rebuild overall guest capacity, cruise lengths, and the number of itineraries and destinations. The key to layering your steps one on the next is to do so one at a time. Only add the next layer once you've confirmed you're able to achieve the one before it. Layering prevents discouragement and builds motivation. Proceed slowly, deliberately, one step at a time. Soon the edge of the fog will be in sight. You'll know what comes next, and you'll have an order of priorities.

3. Probe and Test

In the midst of a crisis, I had a vivid dream in which I was floating in a small, isolated lake high in the mountains. The lake fed several small rivers that flowed in different directions, to different destinations. It was impossible to know which of those rivers was the right one to carry me out of the lake to my hoped-for destination. I would allow myself to be drawn into the headwaters of a river by its current, just far enough to get an idea of what lay ahead, but not so much that I could not furiously paddle my way back to the safety of the lake. I probed each river in this way, thinking, *Which one, which one?* And then I had to make that total commitment to a single direction that is so difficult in uncertain circumstances.

The dream could not have been more clear. It was a reminder that it was time for me to probe the options and to make a committed decision based on the information available. You must do the same. Test the market. Bump up hard against reality for feedback. Leave yourself room to backpedal as you explore each avenue. But then you must choose to enter the stream, be carried forward, and never look back.

4. Seek and Accept Feedback

A cruise ship requires many hands to make a voyage. There are those you are responsible for and accountable to—stakeholders, regulators, employees, management, customers, the general public, your community, and your family. Listen to them. Ask for counsel where appropriate.

In the cruise industry, we ask specific questions of previous guests and prospects about when they would be ready to cruise again and under what conditions. We observe their behavior in the form of information requests and bookings, where we can see precisely the calculus of our customers' purchasing behavior (or lack thereof) as it relates to different destinations, time periods, and cruise lengths.

If you're dealing with a business, career or personal crisis, address those you are closest to who are most impacted. They will help you define the new rules and path to recovery that is on the horizon.

• • • •

Let's look at an example of a cruise line that followed all four steps as they sailed out of the pandemic. A cruise company whose leadership chose to seize the future and become the cruising public's go-to choice for an early return to cruise travel. Since their voyages were North America based, closer to home and not requiring long and complicated international travel, I felt confident that with the right actions, the company could experience a very positive recovery, and more quickly than other cruise lines. In times of disruption, many consumers are willing to travel, but they start with shorter trips that don't take them far from the familiar security of home, family, and medical care, if needed.

All this meant we needed to market the cruises long before they would be taken. We worked on a messaging strategy to encourage people to vacation close to home. Marketing and advertising demonstrated the company's commitment to health and safety so guests could feel safe to travel with confidence during the pandemic.

I laid out a six-month strategy based on the three-step restart plan. The whole project revolved around marketing, sales, and revenue generation. Since we'd done no marketing for months, it was time to start there. We hadn't talked to our past guests or prospective guests. We hadn't talked to travel agents. So we started engaging travelers who were pulled into their turtle shells, waiting for the coast to clear.

We knew people were hesitant to talk about vacations and cruises. We felt we had to give people permission and a reason to dream beyond the virus. A reminder that this situation was not forever. We reengaged their love of travel and offered our calendar of future destinations and new ships.

Another step in this plan was that we changed our policies. Now if, for any reason, customers' plans change or our plans change, they get a full refund of the cruise fare paid, with none of the typical cancellation or administrative fees. It's a no-risk booking environment. This policy created an added safety feature that gave people permission to dream. We wanted to resonate with the people who were eager to be traveling again. We created an atmosphere where it's smart to make commitments out into the future for those dreams because the opportunity may not be there for you later. Not only can you dream, but you can do it without taking uncomfortable risks.

We started with a low funnel strategy. This method was to reach out to past guests who had traveled with us before and those who were booked on one of the cruises that were canceled because of COVID. The strategy was simply to get the people whose plans were dashed to rebook out into the future. They were likely to be eager to have something to look forward to, they had already booked with us previously, and we were very much looking forward to welcoming them aboard and fulfilling their travel dreams.

We followed the three-step plan to a T. We identified our firsts, maintained each as a priority, and adjusted along the way based on feedback. It has been a success by every measure. Once we built momentum and saw bookings come in, we decided to accelerate customer outreach. We went to the next most qualified consumer segment: frequent cruisers. We wanted people excited about cruising again, so we emphasized the new destination possibilities, the new ships, and the new itineraries available in 2022 and even into 2023 with attractive early-booking savings.

By following this proactive plan, entering into 2021 with positive developments unfolding, the company was reaching out into the future beyond the fog to claim their success. Granted, that future was two to three years away; nevertheless, the time would pass. They were ready and committed. Eyes on the prize!

First Firsts to Last Lasts

Individuals struggling in a disruption can also play the long game to win—even if all seems lost in the short term. If the good jobs aren't open, your living situation changes abruptly, or a health crisis threatens everything you hold dear, think through your first first. Then also consider your last last. What do you want your world to look like when the fog is far behind you? You can repeat the first first journaling exercise to brainstorm and prioritize all your last lasts.

Commit the next two to three years (or however long the disruption is projected to last) to studying the future. Your preparation will enable you, your organization, or your family to reach the right place at the right time—all in due time.

Let's say a major event resulted in a steep pay cut. You kept your job but felt like you lost your sense of value and dignity. Consider these numbers: most industries grow at a relatively steady rate of 3 to 4 percent per year. But if your industry or career was severely impacted by a disruption, within two to three years, the recovery rebound can mean 30 percent growth. You'll rarely see that level of rapid opportunity expansion. Everyone in a position to benefit from that rebound will. Stay the course in your industry, earn a promotion, and ask for more stock options instead of a higher salary or bonuses. Soon, those will be worth more than they would have been without the disruption, and the fortune you're sitting on in two to three years may mean you are more secure and perhaps can retire early.

In the broader world beyond work, think about what else is possible for your life, given your knowledge, skills, and abilities. Think about what your next steps could be as you restart from a personal disruption. I've had to do that several times in my life, and I always seem to end up with the same priorities. It may sound selfish, but I always make my health and state of mind my first firsts when I'm thrust into a personal crisis. Without my physical vitality or my mind, I can accomplish nothing for myself or anyone else. The clarity of mind and spirit that comes from a healthy foundation and vital relationships is the key to forging ahead and opening up new choices, no matter the situation you face. Health and vitality are power. Knowledge is power. Powerful people outlast disruption. Every time.

If your first first is finances, do whatever it takes to stabilize the situation. Are you looking to get a new job, to start a business or side hustle, or to take training that sets you up for all the above? It can be difficult to know where to start, I freely admit. With a disruption like COVID-19, many faced their own no-sail restrictions; lockdowns shut doors on businesses in staple industries overnight. How do we keep the lights on when we're prohibited from opening?

While you may not be trying to restart a fleet of cruise ships, the thoughtful step-by-step approach outlined here will work for you as it has for me and my clients over the decades. The level-headed decision to pursue one first at a time and proceed to the next only when you've satisfied the demands of the previous will put you in an advantageous position. Others will be lost in the fog while you accelerate out of it. What if, instead of stressing about how to get back to where you were, you examined the possibilities of the place you're in right now? COVID-19 is a once-in-a-generation opportunity to redefine the future for people who see it as such. That must be your mindset as you plan your restart: What steps can you take in a new direction that might have been impossible without this disruption?

Don't Wait till It's Too Late

You also don't have to wait for a disruption to plan your success. My wife and I have always had a rolling three-year plan; we call it our life plan. We sit together over coffee or a glass of wine as we discuss the upcoming thirty-six months. What do we know about that period? Usually, it's stuff like our son's thirty-fifth birthday or our fortieth wedding anniversary. Frame your three-year period. What do you know about it? And what do you want out of it? What would be your realistic expectations in the next three years?

Usually, my wife and I come up with things like staying healthy, having fun, enjoying more time with our friends and our family, and travel experiences we would like to have together. Then it gets more specific to include things we each individually want to do more of. Pretty soon, we have a context to go by, an understanding of what we will work on together and what we will support each other in as we pursue our individual goals, and a list of what to expect—instead of just reacting to what unfolds. I get a lot of relief from having that big picture. I realize I don't have to accomplish all my wants, needs, and responsibilities in this one moment. I have time and, on a rolling basis, even more time if I need it.

If you're experiencing a setback and your perspective is very short, that setback seems enormous and total. This could send you into a downward spiral of despair, worry, and frustration. If the setback occurs within a bigger, more positive perspective, you've got options. You may have to delay some of your plans, but you know what's a priority.

Lots of people have reached out to me in a personal disruption, like a job loss or a family illness. The one piece of advice I give myself and others during these times is to get right back in motion. If you fall off the bike, get right back on. The bike is always there. The next job is always there. The next endurance race is there. You know those sushi restaurants where the track goes around with different plates of sushi on offering? Life is a continuous buffet. Some of us don't have the confidence that new choices will keep coming around for us. But they surely will.

There isn't a single person who hasn't thought, *I wish I had more time. I would focus on my health. I would learn a new skill. I would create something. I would fix things.* How many incredibly valuable things are always right there waiting for our attention? When you face disruption, why not pick one of those joyous tasks and give yourself the gift of something positive over which you have control? Then you're going to make better quality choices because you'll be in a better place, immersed in something you're passionate about.

Start believing the world's going to have something to offer you, and you're going to be ready. That's the place you want to restart from.

CHAPTER 5

Get Flexible

The Fourth Protocol for Survival, Stability, and Success

Life is a balance of holding on and letting go.

—Rumi

A lot can change in a day.

For me, it was an early morning in the Pacific Northwest. A bit cloudy but a pleasant late summer day of weather emerging. I got in my car and turned on the radio. A commercial faded from focus as I thought about the day's meetings schedule coming up. At the time, I was an executive vice president at Holland America Line. As a subsidiary of Carnival Corporation, we were nearing the end of a strong year of growth, including several "Industry's Best" awards. Our guests rated our crew, ships, and cruise vacations highly, as was the case for all our sister companies within the Carnival family. But "best" wasn't enough.

We constantly strove to raise our own traditions of excellence. New ships, new experiences, new frontiers.

The dozens of details swirling around my head suddenly stopped when the commercial break ended.

"There are reports from New York that an aircraft collided into one of the World Trade Center towers," said the morning show host.

For the next few minutes, the typically clever and upbeat on-air personalities broke character. Instead, they sounded somber. Details were still sparse. They assumed it was an accident, as did I. At that low altitude, the only thing that could have crashed into a building would have to be a small private plane. I recalled once reading about the B-25 bomber airplane that crashed into the Empire State Building at the end of World War II. The crew lost their way in thick fog. History repeats, I thought. But soon it was being reported that it was a large jetliner involved in the crash.

Then came another shock just before I reached the office.

"A second large aircraft just hit the second tower." By then it was apparent these were two commercial passenger jets.

An accidental airplane collision is a tragedy. Two intentional plane crashes into New York City's two tallest buildings sharply and permanently alters the course of human history.

When I arrived at the office, senior management was already gathering around the boardroom TV in absolute silence, watching America's worst nightmare play out—mass murder of civilian men, women, and children on United States soil by adversaries unknown. Around 10:00 a.m., the Federal Aviation Administration (FAA) grounded all commercial flights, an order that redirected over three thousand flights across North America to the nearest airport.[11] This marked the first time in history the FAA stopped all flights.

As the horrific reality unfolded in New York, Pennsylvania, and Washington, DC, the implications reached far. Not only were we faced with a devastating attack the likes of which the modern world had never

---

11   "9/11 Timeline," History.com, last revised September 11, 2020, https://www.history.com/topics/21st-century/9-11-timeline.

seen; we were also out of our depth in the challenges that resulted from it. The travel and tourism industry had no response plan for a sudden system-wide jolt disruption like 9/11. We'd have to be flexible and create one in real time.

First there was the operational impact of taking care of guests and employees and making sure they were all accounted for. The next step was trying to deal with the fact that we couldn't get guests to or from ships—meaning cruises couldn't operate. In Alaska, at least one of our ships was used as a hotel for a few weeks for this very reason—guests couldn't get home. Multiple other ships had to adjust itineraries and change or cancel upcoming cruises. Our customer care team worked overtime, literally night and day, to accommodate and look out for our guests. Flights had to be rebooked; extra days at hotels, motor coach transportation, and meals had to be arranged, all on short notice and at a time when the available options were few. It is amazing what a company culture focused on total guest satisfaction can accomplish under the most challenging of conditions. Never underestimate the power and commitment of your front line team. When their commitments and values are fully aligned and reflective of the company's mission, miracles can and will happen. In fact, that is the only way customer care miracles happen in a people business like the cruise and travel industry. It is a business of passion and love. Many other industries would benefit from a similar approach—especially, in my view, the technology industry. Sometimes you have to wonder where the heart and soul behind the latest apps, software, algorithms, and hardware are.

My journal entry from September 23, 2001, documents the state of the industry.

> For a couple of hours that morning, we were literally under attack. Thousands of commercial and private airplanes were ordered to land immediately, all airports were closed, and fighter jets patrolled the skies. This went on for several days. Meanwhile, the airlines are on the verge of bankruptcy, the stock market crashed, and everyone quit traveling.

The impact on Holland America Line, and all travel companies, has been enormous. Massive cancellations, huge declines in new bookings. We were plunged into a nightmare of disrupted business operations, thousands of customers unable to fly to or from our ships, and the highest level security precautions. Things have only just stabilized, but are far from normal. We are predicting a very challenging period ahead, in which several weaker cruise lines will likely go out of business, and companies like ours may actually lay up some ships for a few months to reduce costs.

These events were beyond comprehension, though perhaps imaginable. In the course of one morning, so much changed. It was made clear that we were not as safe as we had thought, that our economy was more vulnerable than we had thought, and that there was a new type of danger that could live among us and strike without warning.

At Holland America alone, we had nearly fifteen thousand guests scheduled to fly to and from cruise ship departure ports all over the world. Many voyages were canceled, delayed, or sailed with painfully few guests because of those who could not get to the ships.

After the initial shock wave, the next impact was public fear of airplanes and other transportation—including cruise ships. Travelers felt they might be the targets of future attacks. Even when flights and cruises returned to their regular schedules, many American vacationers were hesitant or afraid to go travel until they were convinced the perceived threat to their safety had been resolved. The unthinkable had happened once. No one knew what might happen next.

Then, in October, anthrax attacks on news organizations and elected officials made headlines. Now targeted bioterrorism? And the financial markets roiled with uncertainty about recovery. Many guests who chose to bear with us through the initial events of 9/11 now canceled or changed future trips out of a combination of financial and security concerns.

All these aftereffects lengthened and deepened the disruption. The world was mourning, and we had to be flexible and get creative. Overcoming financial and operational setbacks meant redefining success for the period of disruption. As the cruise industry recovered from the events of 9/11, we at Holland America had a mindset to do the right thing for all our stakeholders, no matter what. We had officers, crew members, and shoreside staff to look out for; guests to protect and serve; and many cancellations and changes to process. We made the choice to be fluid, to adapt to the updated status quo, believing that conditions would ultimately change in our favor and that our actions today would affect the quality of tomorrow.

In the last quarter of 2001, the only way we could move forward was by ascertaining what we could do and trying not to dwell on what we couldn't. To Holland America and to other cruise lines, flexibility meant adjusting to the suddenly changed outlook and preferences of consumers. Meeting them where they were—in every way.

When people don't feel good about what's going on in the world, they stay closer to home, which means they don't book discretionary leisure trips to the far corners of the globe. When people don't feel good about their safety and security, they may cancel bookings, even if there's a cancellation fee. So we worked with customers and made exceptions to our policies. It wasn't a normal situation; normal cancellation fees didn't seem fair. We needed to find a balance between traditional penalties and incentives to stay loyal for future travels. Fail to be flexible and fair under new circumstances and you risk losing the lifetime value of a customer, which, in the case of cruise vacations, could be tens of thousands of dollars per guest.

At Holland America, we always prioritized customer relationships and lifetime customer value but, of course, in ways that also made business sense. An impactful global event can trigger a significant number of cancellations for cruises operating within the known or perceived time horizon during which the event could affect safety, security, or even peace of mind when traveling. In a nightmare scenario, the proverbial "run on the banks" could occur and demand for refunds would exceed cash available to fund them. This was not the case at a large and profitable company like ours, but it is always top of mind in the midst of a big negative event. Thus, there is always a dynamic tension in the decision to enforce or relax a company's cancellation policies, which often involve a fee or charge to the customer. A better option, one that meets the needs of customers and company, is to find a level of incentive that encourages customers to rebook a cruise further into the future, applying the funds they've already paid toward that future cruise, rather than receiving a refund. This results in an interesting partnership between customer and company to get through the disruption together and to look toward brighter days ahead, when the customer can experience that wonderful vacation they were dreaming of in the first place. Our customers understood that we were trying to meet them with reasonable options.

Certainly, if a guest absolutely insisted on a refund and it was within the range of policy, or even relaxed policy, we would do it. But we always encouraged people to take a future cruise credit, not just so they could still enjoy a trip with us, but so they would have something positive to look ahead to, despite the current interruption in their plans. After all, the cruise business is built on a commitment to fulfilling dreams and exceeding expectations, and we were very good at doing just that. We were dealing with a lot of extra expenses associated with disrupted operations, such as chartering airplanes to bring guests and crew home. This type of creative solution helped us focus our cash on solving problems and ensure the quickest possible return to normalized operations.

In uncharted territory, I've learned that the best go-to response protocol is to admit when there isn't one. When faced with an unprecedented situation, you often can't do what you've always done. You must be flexible within the new constraints of the disruption. Be agile and responsive and adapt to the changing nature of the situation while balancing stakeholder priorities. For us, that meant being flexible to help our stranded guests and crew members, responding to customers concerned about future cruises, and adjusting financial projections.

Disruption requires a new approach. Throw out the old playbook. This theme appears in each of the six protocols; however, the *how* of accepting and managing change is an essential best practice, so it deserves its own place alongside the other five protocols.

Four Keys to Get Flexible and Change-Manage Your Way Through Any Crisis

Change management is a term you're familiar with if you've worked in any organization. Even in fair conditions, something's always up: a new client, a new technology, a new team member. Change is ever present. What's different about disruptive change is its many unforeseen consequences. And it cuts deep into your status quo.

In the wake of 9/11, there were many changes in the cruise industry and within our company. By 2004, the International Maritime Organization had implemented sweeping new security regulations designed to protect ships and port facilities, known as the International Ship and Port Facility Security Code or the ISPS Code. An entirely new look at the potential vulnerability of maritime ports and of the massive cruise ships resulted in a more complete understanding of the risks posed by terrorism and ushered in an era of extensive new countermeasures. The ISPS Code prescribed responsibilities to every government authority, port authority, shipping company, and seafarer involved in international voyages. Since the sea is one of the easiest ways to approach an international territory, the ISPS Code mainly looks after the security aspects of the ship, seafarers, ports, and port workers to ensure preventive measures can be taken if a security threat is determined.

Just as sweeping and future looking was the transformation we undertook at Holland America Line to adapt to a new marketplace and new trends that had accelerated post 9/11. The threat of terrorism was top of mind at all times as we worked to implement new and higher levels of security precautions and ease the concerns of customers. For a time, it felt like our collective company ship had a thousand leaks, and we had to move quickly, plugging as many as we could with the resources available. Bail. Steer. Repair. Repeat.

Flexibility enables you to respond successfully so that you're able to outlast disruption and return to port for any necessary repairs—or resume your journey in calmer waters with clearer skies. Here are four ways to remain agile in your response to disruption.

1. Address Critical Issues

Identify the pain points that you need to creatively and quickly relieve, especially when there's no existing protocol for solving those new problems.

In the days and weeks immediately following the 9/11 attacks, we had guests and employees stranded around the globe by the airline lockdown. We had to find ways to keep them safe and comfortable while working with airline partners to bring them home as soon as practicable, and there was no precedent for doing so. Keeping their concerned families and friends assured that these stranded travelers were safe and accounted for and that everything possible was being done to get them home was also an enormous task.

We had to make good, smart, and fast decisions to relieve tens of thousands of people's headaches. All hands were on deck to solve these issues before we could even begin to revise ship schedules and resume normal operations.

Each issue to be addressed, and the action plans to address them, uncovered a host of additional challenges. We could not put any of them off as they would only grow in size and urgency. We had to double down and stay focused. It's like that game Whac-A-Mole. Address the challenges immediately as they become known. Clear the most urgent matters first, whatever it takes, so you can think through what comes next with a clear head and focused attention.

2. Adapt to New Demand Patterns

When you're flexible, you become hyperaware of critical issues that need to be managed. In the cruise industry, the rapid change in consumer preference from international to domestic trips after 9/11 required us to adapt. We had to keep our ships busy, our crews employed, and our guests traveling with us. That meant shifting to align with new customer interest in staying close to home and avoiding airplanes.

At the time, Holland America kept a seasonal itinerary schedule, with most ships in Europe, Alaska, or Asia Pacific, depending on the month. In response to 9/11, we reconfigured the fleet deployment, expanding our cruises from North American home ports dramatically; sending fewer ships to Europe, South America, and Asia; and increasing our capacity in the Caribbean, Mexico, Canada, and Alaska. If we'd repeated the past, we would not have achieved our goals of keeping our ships full, our officers and crews employed, and our guests sticking with us.

When a market niche shrinks, open up the new possibilities. Broaden your horizons. Segmentation taken to the extreme, which is what free markets do, isolates and divides. Shrinks markets rather than expanding them. You must maintain a larger perspective about the market opportunity and resist getting completely consumed by the ever-narrowing funnel of segmentation. It is valuable to a point, but also limiting.

That's why you must stay informed. What do your customers want and need? And are those customers changing? Find out each so you can give it to them—whoever they are—and you will be on the path to recovering the business and once again looking ahead to how to achieve your future goals.

This requires humility above all else. You had great ideas to achieve success before the new normal. It's time to let those go. The wave of emotion is strong, I know. I've been there. It's a hard realization: *what I'm good at isn't working the same as before.*

At least you are not alone. Take the cruise industry amid the coronavirus pandemic. A renewed sense of humility connected beleaguered cruise lines more deeply and positively with their essential partners around the globe: travel agents, ports, personnel agencies, supply chain partners, and shore excursions providers. Our interdependence was made manifest as a result of the pause—and was the obvious key to our restart once new case numbers began to decline.

Where in your business, career, or life would humility connect you with those you depend on for recovery from disruption? It's those individuals or organizations that will enable you to adapt to change, and vice versa. Your enterprise or career is only as resilient as your customers, employees, coworkers, and distribution channel partners. Prioritize these relationships above all else.

3. Adjust for the Long Term

Once you get your bearings in the midst of disruption, you can adapt to the times. Which bumps in the road are here to stay? Which ones will get bigger? In what ways will the status quo likely revert to its pre-disruption state?

For example, fear of terrorism remained for many years after September 11. This disruption brought an ever-present fear that it could happen again at any moment. We saw the TSA change protocols for flights that we still live with today. We also saw standardized cruise ship antiterrorism protocols. There were watch lists to check as people got on any plane or ship. Luggage and guest screening were all new, as were inspection of cargo and harbor sweeps around massive ships. Recently, cruise ship passengers have been targeted while they're ashore. The security bubble keeps expanding. Changing with these expanding concerns is crucial to ongoing growth and success. As circumstances change, make adjustments to remain in demand today, tomorrow, and beyond.

4. Demonstrate That You've Made Positive Changes

When customers, clients, or anyone else whose attention you want is in an altered state, re-engage in new and creative ways. Otherwise, you fade into the background noise—or worse, you appear to have failed to grasp their current mental, emotional, and financial concerns.

Winning back attention in the midst of change involves more than adapting what you offer. You must also stand out from the competing alternatives. At Holland America, we chose to chart post-9/11 cruising differently than our competitors. Instead of sticking with the old play-book, we improved and evolved everything to better fit what customers were looking for. We refocused on our primary goal (our first first)—sustainable success achieved through leadership, innovation, disciplined execution, and profitable operations to secure all our stakeholders for years to come.

How, exactly, did evolving and standing out from the competition achieve that tripart goal? And what, exactly, did that differentiation look like? Perhaps our answers will help you find yours.

How to Differentiate so You Can Flexibly Navigate Disruption

Prior to September 11, the Holland America Line brand proudly prom-ised a tradition of excellence going back 125 years to the company's founding. In the aftermath, we had to make some changes if we were going to recapture customer attention, as every cruise line did. The period of 2001 to 2004 was affected and reshaped by numerous events including 9/11, Afghanistan and Iraq, the economic slowdown, the stock market decline and lower consumer confidence, new travel inconve-niences related to security, the airline industry in crisis, and SARS and norovirus, plus unprecedented capacity growth in the form of a mas-sive order book of new ships by virtually all cruise lines. Capacity was expanding at a much faster pace than demand, given the negative impact of so many types of disruption in one concentrated period of time.

Companies in the cruise industry were competing over too few cus-tomers, given the relentless capacity expansion driven by new ships. Once we got those customers, we wanted to keep them. That meant updating the Holland America promise to broaden our appeal beyond longtime guests and older customers who longed for the way things were—for tradition.

In the years following 9/11, I helped lead Holland America through a transformation—from "Tradition of Excellence" to "Signature of Excellence." The initiative brought an investment of over $500 million over time in what we called the five pillars of excellence. I think of our work at Holland America as an adaptable framework anyone can use for their own voyage of transformation. It offers everyone a model for differentiation in whatever situation you're experiencing disruption in—an industry, a business venture, a personal challenge, anything.

"Signature of Excellence" is how we reclaimed the future for a long-established global brand that was being disrupted by events, time, traditions, competition, and changing consumer preferences.

This framework begins with discovering the clear-eyed truth about what you have to work with. In our case, the five pillars detailed different aspects of the customer experience. As the image below shows, our approach to premium cruising excellence revolved around dining, ships and accommodations, customer service, activities, and destinations.

Signature of Excellence Initiative

You can use this same model in any disruption you face. In business and in your personal life, you must change with the times because what worked before the disruption rarely endures intact afterward.

I recommend choosing your own four to seven pillars of excellence that will enable you to stand out from the pack. There's something special about the number five. It's small enough to focus on the important things yet large enough to include all the essentials.

In this example, each pillar upheld the customer experience, but behind the scenes were also a number of initiatives associated with company culture, vessel design, operational excellence, technology enhancements, financial optimization, marketing, and distribution. For a company that sells a physical product, quality control and craftsmanship would be the focus. Happy customers are the best salespeople, after all. A company's five pillars might be product performance, product reliability, product safety, satisfaction guarantee, and innovation. For a freelancer who offers a service, client retention could be the priority. It's significantly easier to keep a client than to onboard a new one. Your six pillars could be customer satisfaction, high quality of service, added value beyond expectation, timeliness of service, reliability of service, and deep relationships with each of your customers that enable you to listen and anticipate needs. And an individual reentering the dating pool might prioritize physical appearance and mastering social skills. Their six pillars might be health and physical fitness, being informed and thoughtful about current events, a wardrobe that suggests style and confidence, ability to listen, reliability, and trustworthiness. You can apply the signature-of-excellence approach to any industry, business, or individual.

Let's pull the spyglass up to personal disruptions for a moment. At Holland America, we had thousands of employees to execute our initiative. As a person, it's . . . just you. In any disruption when you're feeling stuck, at the end of the day, you have to provide yourself with a new purpose and focus. And you have to provide the world with new reasons to take a fresh look at you, to listen to what you have to say, and to look at what you have to offer. Whether it's your skills, your health, or your relationships, your personal signature of excellence enables you to clarify and effectively communicate who you are and what you have to offer.

The last thing you want to do in the fog is come across as lost in it. Overwhelmed. Out of touch. Irrelevant. This goes for individuals and for industry. Competition is ever present everywhere. Act like it. Now, that doesn't mean somebody has to win, and somebody has to lose. It means you're aware of the alternative viable choices that your potential customers, employers, or suitors have available to them.

Competition even exists in goal setting. In a health crisis, your enemy is self-sabotage, competing against yourself. You might even have people in your life who are subconsciously dragging you down for pursuing change. For example, when I decided to begin training for Ironman triathlons, some people close to me didn't like the fact that I was changing my lifestyle, that I was more focused on health than they were, or that my free time was devoted to training and learning the sport. All of a sudden, I realized who was supporting me and who was undermining me. It's the same with positioning yourself inside a company for a promotion. Disruption reveals who the real competition is for that moment in time. Those who make it out of the fog will be those willing to chart a zigzag course. So put in the work. Strengthen your advantages. Earn attention. Different, done right, is better.

It may not be easy to define your pillars of excellence. To discover the truth about where you are right now and what your strengths and weaknesses are, here's some guidance to close that gap.

Six Questions to Construct Your Pillars of Excellence

Pillars vary for each business or individual, even those in direct competition with you. No one is exactly like you. How are your differences excellent? Ask yourself these six questions to point you toward your pillars. Adapt these to be more specific to your situation.

1. What's the truth about your current market?
2. What's the truth about your brand and how well it aligns with core market trends?

3. How does what you offer meet your customer's expectations in relation to your competition?
4. What's the truth about this disruption's impact moving forward?
5. What should you be focusing on right now?
6. What should you be preparing for further out into the future?

After the questions are asked, prioritize your answers into actions you can take. Out of the hundreds of post-9/11 improvement recommendations Holland America leadership received from customers, employees, and consultants, *all* of them supported one big promise: an industry-leading premium customer experience. Our promise was bound up in our mission: "Holland America is the premium cruise line for those seeking an enriching cruise experience delivered in a 'classic and timeless' style."

Consider recent examples of effective, differentiated promises from cruise lines in the midst of the coronavirus pandemic. The forward-looking optimism of the cruise industry is remarkable. It is how cruise lines consistently engage guests in a partnership of anticipation and continuous renewal. Here are a few examples from the most recent issues of *Departures* magazine: Regent Seven Seas asks, "Do You Feel It? The World Is Getting Closer." Silversea asks, "What Lies Beyond the Edge?" Oceania Cruises encourages, "Remember the Future." Seabourn invites, "Rediscover Extraordinary Worlds." Beyond magazines, a Disney Cruise Line TV spot reminds, "Dreams Do Come True." Plus, two of my personal favorites—Victory Cruise Lines asks, "Where Will You Be When the World Reopens?" And American Queen Steamboat Company invites, "Come Home to America in 2021." That is how an industry places itself on the leading edge of recovery, time and again.

American Queen went so far as to acquire the shore excursion company that provides most of its experiences ashore for customers, enabling the company to develop even more unique experiences and control the quality of all. This, even as the cruise industry remained on pause, unable to operate cruises.

Clearly, differentiation is not only about what's changed; it's about who you need to be as a result of this change. How do you need to change with it to keep the promise that matters most? You must be responsive to the changing situation, which means you need to note what this disruption has changed permanently or for the near future.

At Holland America, we needed to have stronger reasons for somebody to choose us instead of another brand. We needed to be able to more clearly describe the overall premium experience of cruising with us. And, of course, we had to provide that experience in a way that made guests feel safe and worry free while adapting to a litany of new regulations. We met customers where they were with new, more accessible, closer-to-home cruise vacation alternatives.

After completing the framework and reestablishing priorities with the five pillars, we designed our future ships differently. They were designed to attract a broader audience of customers and to operate more cost efficiently. They were designed to give us the flexibility of going back and forth between the seven-day Caribbean cruise and the twelve- to fourteen-day European cruise. Yes, we did need to sail across the oceans again after 9/11, and soon. Differentiation first meant bringing customers back onto our ships in complete safety, then offering them the experience of a lifetime so they would sail again with us.

That's why flexibility was designed into our fleet and into our operations so that we could succeed under multiple different scenarios. We learned from 9/11 that our future is never secure. Being one kind of cruise company was not safe because of the international flight stoppage. So we adjusted. And the signature of excellence initiative ensured that we changed for the better across the board.

You can only succeed if you're willing to be flexible and adapt to a changing market, as well as having priorities in place so you know what matters. Then every time something happens—whether it's SARS, September 11, COVID-19, or a personal disruption—you're going to handle what you're faced with and shift yourself out of the fog. There's no going back, so make sure your actions put you on a course forward to the best possible destination. As former Intel CEO Andy Grove said, "Bad companies are destroyed by crises; good companies survive them; great companies are improved by them."

CHAPTER 6

Become Collision Proof

The Fifth Protocol for Survival, Stability, and Success

The greatest test of courage on earth is to bear defeat without losing heart.
—Robert Green Ingersoll

When I was just two years old, my mother left. I wouldn't see her again for thirty years.

My parents were teenagers when they married. At age nineteen, they had my sister. Two years later, I arrived. When my mother abandoned the family, it was sudden. One day, she was there. The next, she was gone. Her departure left a twenty-three-year-old single father to raise two toddlers. I was definitely born into a path of disruption.

This awesome responsibility had a big impact on my dad's outlook on life. He dedicated himself to working and striving in order to protect and provide. He came from a challenging childhood himself and had nothing to go forward with other than his own initiative and work ethic. And his were enormous, born of necessity and a unique constitution of intelligence, energy, drive, and natural leadership traits.

We lived our early years in Alaska, where I was born. My father came to Alaska working construction on the Alaska Highway project and then began a career in politics and the airline industry. He was elected to the first Alaska State Legislature in 1959. We traveled with the legislative sessions between Fairbanks and Juneau, the state capitol. His airline career quickly progressed, and he became a senior executive of an upstart entrepreneurial airline, Alaska Airlines, which would later become one of the airline industry powerhouses. Our formative years revolved around the chaos of business. My dad was a business builder, an innovator, and a take-no-prisoners type of leader, with a commanding presence, a larger-than-life energy, and his eyes always on the future.

Despite my dad's self-generated initiative, he depended on other people to help raise his two kids. He relied separately on my grandmother, my grandfather, my aunts and uncles, his friends, employees, and even industry acquaintances to watch us. We were often watched over by airline staff, playing behind the ticket counters or in the aircraft hangars. My sister and I got passed around from household to household, location to location, even as far away as Panama. We were adept at flying unaccompanied, navigating the unfamiliar settings, and looking out for each other. Ours was a childhood of continuous disruption. We had to be quick on our tiny feet to adapt to all the changes.

There were times my father's dysfunctional siblings and their children all lived with us under one roof. Drug addiction, alcoholism, and emotional instability among these people were front-and-center early childhood lessons. For my dad, this situation worked of necessity; he was rarely present because of travels and work, so my sister and I could blend into the larger family. And it was great for his siblings because their hardworking "provider" brother supplied a roof over their heads, fed their kids, and paid the bills. Even at an early age, I knew the difference between those who take without giving and those who produce. Our grandmother was a religious zealot who subjected us to a lot of strange and angry experiences. Our grandfather (who had long since divorced our grandmother) was kind, fun, hard living, and tough as nails. Of course, time with Grandpa Joe was our favorite respite within the rotation among troubled adults. Amid the chaotic circumstances, my sister and I operated as a unit. We navigated all turbulence together, instinctively.

Suffice it to say that my most formative years were far from stable and nurturing, but they played a fundamental role in my life skills of focus, anticipating risk, navigating chaos, and coming out with a determination that tomorrow will be better. Eventually, life stabilized. When I was thirteen, our father remarried. Our stepmother brought the first normalcy my sister and I had ever known. But by then, we were grown up, having been raised in business . . . by business . . . for business. When my dad had nowhere to send me, which was more often then he would've liked to admit, he took me with him. I was a young Mini-Me. He built relationships and made deals for hours at restaurants or offices. I sat there quietly with my little bow tie, watching, listening, learning. Witnessing the building of Alaska Airlines from its roots as a regional carrier to its entry into the jet age and destinations beyond was an intensive study in what to do and what not to do.

I know that doesn't sound like much of a childhood, but I see myself the same way I see all change. The good and the bad is all the same—it is the stuff of life. Disruption brings opportunity. I lived a businessperson's life as a child. I learned about entrepreneurship and its complex ties to human nature, how vision and strategy become reality, how interactions between people work, what the pecking order of power really is, and how to expect the unexpected.

Two years after my dad remarried, our family travel (and, eventually, cruise) business was born. By the age of thirteen, I was already working in the travel industry, spending my summers in Southeast Alaska working at a remote fishing lodge, scrubbing and fueling the boats, hauling luggage and gear, and eventually guiding guests on salmon fishing outings. At age seventeen, what would become the family business launched when my father acquired several tourism programs from Alaska Airlines and went out on his own. It was just the four of us: Dad, our stepmother, my sister, and me. All hands on deck. No plan B. Sink or swim. It was serious business, big responsibility, and total accountability. We worked totally and relentlessly in and on the business. By then, I wasn't my father's obligation; I was his business partner in the making. In time, we developed a fantastic relationship. We were yin and yang. As the mad genius, my dad brought chaos wherever he went in business. He left a wide swath of scorched earth wherever he went. I became the cleanup master who brought focus and order to many of his initiatives, and I repaired or smoothed over the ruffled feathers and hurt feelings of those in his path. We shared a purpose, and together, as a family of four, we built our business into a sizable and respected enterprise.

In the first fifteen years of my career, working alongside my parents and sister, I learned the hard lessons and realities of vision, creativity, collaborative effort, business building, risk-taking, financial reward and loss, problem-solving, leadership, disruption, and so on. I attended and graduated from the University of Hard Knocks. Those formative years shaped my thirty-plus-year career helping to build and expand the global cruise and travel industry. Today, I draw on those experiences to help others.

We opened up remote areas of Alaska to authentic and inspiring tourism experiences. The Arctic—Nome, Kotzebue, Point Barrow, and Prudhoe Bay. Also, the remote Pribilof Islands, the "Galapagos of the North," off the Aleutian chain. We took enormous risks chartering and guaranteeing seats on 737 jets to put in place flight schedules that enabled summer-long tour packages. We contracted and owned hotel accommodations and worked with regional Alaska Native corporations to create attractions such as the Museum of the Arctic and with local entrepreneurs to provide experiences such as skin boat rides amid the frozen ice of the Arctic Sea; exploring the stunning miniature ecology of the frozen tundra; gold panning; sampling muktuk, an Eskimo delicacy; and thrilling dogsled rides with real working huskies. We purchased and modified four-wheel-drive school buses and flew them to remote areas in cargo planes, in order to provide transportation and sightseeing in these far remote corners of Alaska. Our rallying cry was "Experience the Real Alaska."

We acquired and operated the national park concession at Glacier Bay National Park in Southeast Alaska and arranged daily jet transportation between Juneau and Gustavus to enable a steady flow of visitors to Glacier Bay Lodge, where we operated cruises to the massive tidewater glaciers, plus sportfishing and naturalist presentations about the vast marine life, wildlife, and glaciers. Glacier Bay became one of the most famous destinations in Alaska, and we played a big part in making that happen.

We developed the first small-ship cruising experiences in Alaska, creating a fleet of American-built and crewed ships with capacity for just under a hundred guests each that visited the deepest nature areas of Alaska's Inside Passage—cruising the deep fjords, right to the face of giant glaciers, and visiting the most remote, historic, and colorful communities—beyond the reach of the large cruise ships.

Recently, I spoke with the head of another pioneering Alaska family based in Fairbanks, where I was born (at that time in the Territory of Alaska, before statehood). Fairbanks is an amazing frontier town on the edge of vast wilderness. My friend's family has operated hardworking paddle-wheel riverboats on the rivers of interior Alaska for five generations. Today, they provide an amazing adventure cruise on the Chena and Tanana Rivers near Fairbanks to hundreds of thousands of visitors each summer. We spoke about COVID and the impact of the entire 2020 and possibly 2021 Alaska tourism seasons being canceled. He said, "It's the first time in seventy years that the paddles haven't turned." That struck me as hard as any description yet of the impact of a full stop on the travel industry and business owners like this great family. We also spoke about looking ahead to the other side of the storm, and his response was equally impactful. "We see things through the lens of a five-generations business. We've been through a lot, and we know how to survive and rebuild."

Here's a tip as you are reading this—imagine the grit required to forge a five-generation business out of the frontier of Alaska and the confidence and perspective that provides you with when going through disruption. What is your source of strength to tap into when the going is tough?

Because of the seasonality of Alaska, combined with the expanding size of our business, the capital invested in our ships (mobile assets), and the cash flow required to sustain it all and to keep growing, we looked to the south for warmer winter destinations and the offsetting revenue opportunities they offered. We developed and pioneered new cruise routes, expanding our vision and the concept of small-ship cruising: "Cruise Special Worlds the Big Ships Can't." This effectively required added layers of capital risks, business risks, and operating risks, one after another, in order to mitigate and address the original risk of Alaska's short and concentrated operating season. (Be careful to take into consideration all the implications of your strategy!) However, in taking these risks, we pioneered and created new small-ship cruising destinations—Columbia/Snake Rivers, the San Juan Islands and the southern coast of British Columbia, the Sea of Cortez, Panama/Costa Rica, Tahiti/French Polynesia, and the US and British Virgin Islands. We cut a huge swath and laid the foundation for a large part of today's small-ship cruise industry.

And those were just the first and early years of my career. Again, it was a crash course in business, risk, disruption, survival, recovery, and continual reinvention.

We were a proud and feisty family enterprise among the emerging giants—Carnival, Royal Caribbean, Princess, Holland America. I could not have foreseen then that I was on a course to one day actually work with those giants, expanding cruising of all types worldwide, and to serve a term as chairman of the global cruise industry association, CLIA.

I've ridden out two cyclones in the Pacific. (They are called hurricanes in the Atlantic.) One was off the eastern coast of Australia aboard a large cruise ship. The other was aboard one of my family's small cruise ships operating in French Polynesia. It may seem counterintuitive, but the safest course of action when a storm approaches is to leave a seemingly safe harbor and ride out the storm on open seas in order to avoid being blown or dashed ashore. There are more options for surviving the storm when you leave the harbor and, in this case, the reef surrounding the island. The massive power of such storms makes clear your smallness and the fragile nature of life. It is something you never forget.

Along this wild journey, I married and began to raise a family of my own. I managed to create a sense of personal stability that I didn't have as a child, and I've been very protective of that state of being for myself and my own family. However, even with my heightened vigilance, disruption proved never far away. Because I have faced disruptions my whole life, it has become innate to me to always be prepared. Experience has taught me that changes happen when you least expect them. You could get that gut-wrenching phone call at any time.

To this day, my family is well-trained in emergency preparedness. We have a master plan for contacting each other in an absolute worst-case scenario. Financial resources, lawyers, insurance, bankers, and other contingency plans remain at the ready as well. Every member of my family has somebody to call when they need to, whether for a personal crisis or a business disruption. We've witnessed plenty of both. Remember the buyout of my family business? When everything we'd invested in and sacrificed for depended on that deal, it collapsed. I felt like I'd been crushed by an eight-hundred-pound gorilla. My life's work obliterated. It was rough, but we made it through.

Since then, disruptions that came out of nowhere have shaped my career. From the roles I've held at cruise companies to the consulting clients I've worked with, I've been a person others look to when a storm hits—whether we're embracing disruption as an opportunity or recovering from being upended by it. Over the years, we've had our unfair share of disruption. And here I've been, in the center of many of them—wars, financial crises, global threats, natural disasters, and cruise ship misadventures. Take a look at this time line going back four decades in my career, which started at a young age.

1980	Mount Saint Helens volcano eruption
1985	*Achille Lauro* hijacking
1987	Black Monday market crash
1989	San Francisco earthquake
1989	US invasion of Panama
1990–1991	Recession
1991	Persian Gulf War I (Kuwait)

1992	Hurricane Andrew
1997	Asia financial crisis
1999–2000	Y2K
2000	Dot-com bubble
2001	Seattle earthquake
2001	9/11
2002	Market downturn
2002–2003	SARS-1
2003	Persian Gulf War II (Iraq)
2005	*Seabourn Spirit* pirate attack
2005	Hurricane Katrina
2007	*Empress of the North* grounding
2007–2009	The great recession
2009–2010	H1N1 (swine flu)
2010	Iceland volcano eruption
2012	*Costa Concordia* disaster
2013	*Carnival Triumph* fire and stranding
2015	Terrorist attack on Costa cruise passengers
2015–2016	European refugee crisis
2015–2016	Market sell-off
2019	*Viking Sky* storm stranding
2020	COVID-19 market crash
2020–2021	COVID-19

For some, these events were passing headlines. *Huh? . . . Wow . . . that really happened? Interesting.* Disruptions like 9/11 and COVID-19 devastated many, of course. But only a tiny share of the global population was directly impacted by terrorism or viruses. At its worst, the novel coronavirus brought fatal symptoms to 6.2 percent of those infected.[12] In no way do these numbers make light of the unimaginable suffering of loved ones. The point of these numbers is their scale. Most

---

12 "Country-by-Country Data on Mortality Risk of the COVID-19 Pandemic," Our World in Data, last revised February 21, 2021, https://ourworldindata.org/mortality-risk-covid.

disruptions capsize the lives of a select number of people relative to the total population.

This is not the case in the cruise industry. Few other businesses require as fair a weather condition as ours. Fair weather politically, financially, naturally—you name it, we need it to go well so we can do business on a worry-free, enjoyable basis for our customers. With such an extensive global footprint, the industry risk is diversified, but every ripple has the potential to become a tsunami. If we lack the will to remain standing, to reemerge from each storm, then we might as well throw in the towel.

Looking through that list of industry events, natural disasters, and other disruptions that have colored my career, I see that my entire life has been one disruption after another. And that's why I relate immediately to anyone in crisis, disruption, or change. I've been there. Every fiber of my being has. It's bittersweet. An upbringing surrounded by disruption and an adulthood defined by it mean I can help people, companies, and even myself avoid ruin when disruption comes. To outlast these disruptions, I've needed to grasp the situation quickly, discern the next best actions, and get everyone out of panic mode and focused on stabilization and recovery.

One disruption on that list that most people generally aren't familiar with affected the cruise industry in my home state of Alaska. In the early hours of May 14, 2007, *Empress of the North* ran aground twenty miles southwest of Juneau.[13] A crew member made a navigational error that could not be rectified in time. The ship ran aground on a remote and dangerous reef in the deep darkness of night, surrounded by icy waters. It had a gash in the hull and was taking on water, and, though stuck on the reef, it was in a precarious, unstable condition, with over two hundred guests and crew who had to be evacuated quickly.

---

13   "NTSB: Master's Poor Decision Led to Grounding of *Empress of the North*," The Maritime Executive, January 10, 2011, https://www.maritime-executive.com/article/2008-07-24-ntsb-masters-poor-decision-led-to-grounding-of-empress-of-the-north.

When something like this occurs, there are those designated parties and people who receive first notice. Of course, the US Coast Guard and any nearby vessels and coastal communities with access to rescue vessels. Also, those who are responsible for managing a company through an incident like this: the incident response team. Ensuring that all possible measures are taken and continue in force to ensure the safety of those involved and then a number of other priorities. I was a key person who got that first notice.

When you lead a cruise line, you sleep with one eye open. Your ships and all aboard them are always out there somewhere, often in remote locations. They're completely dependent on their link back to the land-based organization and support under normal circumstances and especially when things go wrong. As the head of that organization, I was never unreachable. Always, I was available to ensure that every development got addressed quickly and successfully. It could be a mishap as scary as an engine room fire, engine trouble, or simply missing a scheduled port call because of severe weather and headwinds. Sometimes a ship would need to be repaired, a monumental disruption by itself.

Running aground and getting stuck in the middle of frigid seas, forcing elderly people to abandon ship in the middle of the night, is an entirely different emergency. Adrenaline coursed through me when I received that 1:00 a.m. phone call.

Mayday rescue vessels were already en route to the icy straits outside Glacier Bay National Park. Passengers and crew members were evacuated safely without injuries. The vessel sustained damage to its starboard underside and propulsion system. With emergency on-site support taken care of, we now had to assess the damage—and its ramifications on guests, the environment, the company, and the ship itself. We had to formulate a public company response. Fortunately, the captain was able to debrief me before I heard from the media. Since few had firsthand knowledge of the situation, everyone came to me in the hours that followed. Journalists, yes, but also senior executives, management, investors, our PR team, and other staff members. Most were understandably panicked, terrified, or both. This fear response, while natural, was not helpful.

A lifetime of experience kicked in as I activated the company's incident response plan, the most important document to have in the midst of disruption. An incident response plan is just what it sounds like—a step-by-step guide to follow in case of emergency. It includes who to contact and when, who is responsible for what, and which actions to take in what order to deal with the unexpected disruption. It was obviously too late to prevent the misfortune. But we didn't wallow in blame or beat ourselves up with regret. There's plenty of time for investigation and analysis of what went wrong, and why, later. Instead, we snapped into action and followed protocol.

Having that written plan meant we could all do something productive right away. We didn't have to react blindly, even though the event was unexpected. I couldn't be on location, and I didn't know exactly what the outcome would be, but I could put our plan into motion, mitigate catastrophe, and calm the panic. It also helped us respond to the media and others concerned. Because we could speak quickly and honestly with confidence about the steps we were taking, most fear was quickly mitigated and transformed to positive action.

In the meantime, we followed steps to gather and disseminate information. We were very fortunate that no one was seriously injured. Everyone on the ship was taken to Juneau and provided accommodations, medical care, transportation, and constant updates.

After all passengers and crew members were accounted for on shore, we had to deal with the ship, which was still stuck in the straits. The ship was supposed to be finishing a cruise, then starting a new one in four days with hundreds of people booked and ready to travel. Talk about a cascade of negative impacts.

Within a few days, those who were immediately affected were safe, secure, and headed for home. Once the ship was taken to a shipyard for inspection and repair, the US Coast Guard and our own operations team began the investigation. All this took time and hard work. But our incident response plan allowed us to act fast and decisively. We knew exactly what to do to address the situation, contain and address the impact on our company, and meet the needs and concerns of current and future customers as much as possible given the course of events. Our incident response plan, written long before the *Empress* ran aground, was essential and made all the difference in taking the right actions throughout the incident.

Becoming Collision Proof

In most businesses, particularly travel, we see increased priority given to the concept of sustainability. Often that refers to environmental sensitivity and resource conservation, protecting perishable environments and resources. But there is more required in my view. Sustainability must also include removing vulnerabilities, making us more resilient. In a word, becoming antifragile.

Collision proofing is a two-step process, the first of which we've just touched on—having a response to disruption that ensures you're not destroyed. The second, even more critical aspect is planning to avoid collisions in the first place. That's risk management, which we'll come back to later. For now, let's continue with . . .

Incident Response Plan

No matter what you do, you won't always have smooth sailing. If you accept that a disruption is inevitable, you can plan for it. Think of your incident response plan as a trauma response plan. When disruption arrives unexpectedly, as it does, you're not going to eliminate the immediate consequences. At best, if you can act quickly enough, you may be able to stop the initial impact from getting worse. But, at least, you will have a place to start.

Your incident response plan is a comprehensive guide everyone can follow whenever calamity strikes. Emphasis on *everyone*. Incident response plans require all hands on deck. Everyone who is involved must know exactly what their job is and what will be done overall to mitigate the effects as quickly as possible. The practical reason for "all hands on deck" is obvious. More hands mean more help. The other reason your plan needs everyone's buy-in is emotional. The closest thing to peace of mind people have during a disruption is to have a job to do. Empower everyone to be helpful rather than to sit helplessly and spiral into worry. You're acting as a team to respond as quickly and effectively as possible.

The first time I saw an incident response plan put into action, it didn't eliminate the disaster or its effects. But it did tell everyone what to do so they had a purpose amid nearly unspeakable tragedy.

When I was fifteen, my father was still a senior executive at Alaska Airlines. A few months after my fifteenth birthday, we witnessed the worst aviation disaster in American history up to that time. On September 4, 1971, an Alaska Airlines Boeing 727 "crashed into a sheer wall of mountain," my father said when the *New York Times* reached out for a statement.[14] All 109 people on board perished.

Because of my close-up view of my dad's work life, I witnessed firsthand an entire corporation jump into motion around catastrophe. They had an incident response plan, and my father and his team implemented it. They even modified it, making decisions and taking actions right for the moment in a situation larger than such a plan in those days could fully cover. No plan on paper could have made up for the reality of the mass loss of life. An event of this magnitude hadn't happened before in the commercial airline industry, much less at Alaska Airlines. The tragedy played a major role in upgrading flight safety procedures and navigation devices throughout aviation and the response to future incidents. The aircraft went missing on approach to landing at Juneau, Alaska. My father happened to be in Juneau at the time. He was among the first to the crash site, in the mountains eighteen miles from Juneau. It was a devastating and traumatic experience that had a lifelong impact on him. I'll never forget the effects of what is now called post-traumatic stress on his persona. Anxiety, sleeplessness, rapid talk, and then the

---

14   "All 109 Are Killed as Jetliner Hits Alaska Mountain," *New York Times*, September 5, 1971, www.nytimes.com/1971/09/05/archives/all-109-are-killed-as-jetliner-hits-alaska-mountain-727-had-been.html.

inability to talk about it openly and, finally, an urgency to live every moment of life to the fullest. Despite the personal impact, he found deep reserves of strength to provide comfort and leadership to others throughout the incident and its aftermath. Normally, my father's emanating energy affected everyone around him. That tragedy and loss of life affected my dad personally. To this day, I remember the searing intensity and hardship of that event. I heard him describe the accident scene and the sights he encountered there, and I will never forget those impressions. I will forever appreciate that we are all human, and when faced with a great challenge or tragedy, our own humanity is deeply affected. Most will rise to the moment selflessly and then carry the scars of trauma stoically into the future. A lesson—disruption affects everyone involved. Have empathy.

Inevitably, that early trauma shaped my own reactions to later incidents like the *Empress of the North*. My father's saving grace was the incident response plan. Written "do this, then that" guidelines kept the entire organization on a path to do the right things at the right time, in the midst of an earth-shattering event. Addressing the tragedy and then moving through grief, healing, and eventually, closure.

This and other disruptions I saw early in life taught me that those who make it out of the fog always have a plan of action. That's why everyone needs an incident response plan, organizations and individuals alike. To become collision proof means taking action *before* the disruption.

Writing Your Incident Response Plan

The incident response plan is your go-to document so that when something does happen, you're able to steer through the event. The incident response plan you write (and execute when need be) will probably be nowhere near as complex as the plan my father followed at Alaska Airlines or as detailed as the one I followed for *Empress of the North*. But yours will include all the steps that are essential to your situation. Anyone responsible for anything in your plan should have a copy of it.

Many of us have a type of personal incident response plan called a last will and testament. And maybe even a health directive. But life is about more than death, and your likelihood of multiple life disruptions is equally as certain as the eventuality of activating your will. Broaden your thinking and tool kit to include a personal incident response plan to call on when you need it.

As the leader of an organization, you might prepare for an accident at work, the loss of a fundamental employee, a substantial financial loss, or something that results in terrible press for the company. In your personal life, you might prepare for a serious injury or illness, the loss of a loved one, a fire that destroys your home, or losing your job. For some, a family incident response plan makes more sense as many of the risks and actions are the same. These plans help detail what outcomes are expected and what responsibilities everyone has. Once you have a personal incident response plan, make sure your family, closest friends, and advisers all have a copy or know where to find it. While some categories will be different in a personal and professional incident response plan, all plans will help you become collision proof.

When you're shocked by an unexpected disruption, it helps to have a plan already in place so you can take action without delay.

Take a look at the incident response plan we followed the night *Empress of the North* ran aground. Use it as your template and your inspiration, then sit down and create your own plan.

As you read, take notes to start to identify your own vulnerabilities and list realistic ways to avoid peril.

Cruise Company—Incident Response Plan

It is the policy of Cruise Company to be prepared to provide assistance to operating units confronted with crisis situations. Such events may range from a weather-related incident, technical problem or accident, ship grounding, fire, pollution incident or any other incident that could endanger onboard guests, employees or company guests. This procedure assigns responsibility for responding to operational emergencies involving company resources using an **Incident Command System (ICS)**.

Scope

Cruise Company has a number of operating units. A concerted effort is made to ensure each operation is conducted in the safest manner possible. Regardless, there exists the possibility that events will occur that require the organization to provide significant support to assist an operating unit confronted with an emergency. Since the source and effects of the incident are not predictable, it is necessary to create an organization that will ensure a prompt and effective response regardless of the situation.

The **ICS** provides a response structure with titles and job tasks to avoid the interface problems between organizations that can cause confusion and communications problems during an incident. The loss of, or serious disruption to, any critical function can have a significant impact on an organization, in some cases threatening its very survival.

The overriding objective is to ensure that an organization can provide an acceptable level of service to all stakeholders, including customers and other business partners, regardless of any disruptive events or incidents that might occur. Achieving this at reasonable cost and within reasonable timescales are key requirements.

Reportable Incidents

The definition of a "Reportable Incident" is any situation where there is a possible, provable or definite injury, loss of life or injury/loss of company property and/or injury/loss to the environment. This includes any business interruption that results in monetary or customer confidence loss. When any of the aforementioned incidents occur, we are bound to move into the defined roles.

Note: In the event of a Reportable Incident all individuals are to be prepared immediately to take action. All individuals should keep a copy of this policy at home, in the office and reachable within a moment's notice.

Structure for Use "at Time of Incident"

An Incident Response Plan is seen as a living document that will change as the organization and personnel changes occur. For the purpose of Cruise Company's Plan we are taking a 3-tiered approach to incident management following strategic, tactical, and operational aspects.

Phone Tree

At the point of a Reportable Incident, the individuals listed will be alerted as indicated with the arrows. The President must be notified immediately.

The Phone Tree process is impeded if the President is not notified immediately following an incident. He or she will dictate how far down the phone tree the calls will be made. The President will immediately assume the role of **Headquarters Incident Commander (HIC)**, which also includes Company Spokesperson.

Incident Response Plan

The following constitutes the steps that are to be followed and managed in tandem with the Headquarters Incident Commander and the Tactical and Operational teams when alerted an Incident has taken place or is in process. The steps are as follows:

1. Ascertain the details of the incident. Respond with urgency to all injuries or possible/probable loss of life by calling proper authorities. Formulate decisions as to the scope of the Incident.
2. Ensure immediate contact has been made with the President. He assumes the role of Headquarters Incident Commander at this time.
3. Initiate the phone tree.
4. Provide go-forward instructions to the Field Incident Commander.
5. Secure scene. Ask the representative at Incident site to respond to inquiries by individuals, the press or government

by making a non-emotional request that they contact the company President.

6. Contact Attorney and Insurance Provider, as needed.
7. Communicate with Employees. Provide instructions for handling all incoming phone calls and inquiries regarding the incident.
8. Communicate with Guests, and Emergency Contacts of Guests, as needed.
9. Contact Public Relations firm, as needed.
10. Write statement of facts and statement for the Press.
11. Release statement to the Press and employees.
12. Arrange Press meeting. Hold Press Conference. Meet with employees.
13. Manage process until the scene is secure and the incident has passed.
14. Communicate the releasable results of the incident.
15. Make corrections on any areas that were deemed unsafe.
16. Hold final informational Q&A with employees and the Press, if applicable.
17. After the incident is over, meet as a Recovery Team and discuss those areas in need of improvement.

Incident Commander and Command Center

When President, the Headquarters Incident Commander (HIC), has decided to activate the Headquarters Incident Command Center, the Phone Tree will be activated.

Following the instruction from the HIC, all department heads will ensure that support staff members considered necessary are contacted immediately, notified of occurrence and advised of what is required of them. These essential individuals are expected to report to the Headquarters Incident Command Center at the earliest possible time.

Tactical—Management/Response Team Members

The following individuals (list) are members of the Incident Response Team at the tactical level. These individuals should be contacted in the event of a disaster of any proportion so that they can make the proper assessment and alert the Headquarters Incident Commander.

Recovery Team

The following individuals (list) are members of the Incident Recovery Team. These individuals should be contacted in the event of a disaster of any proportion so that they can make the proper assessment and alert the Headquarters Incident Commander.

Press Management—(Release of Printable Facts)

News travels fast, and it seems that bad news travels faster. And if the bad news is about an incident involving the company, the media could be at the site before we are ready to respond.

The way we respond to the media and release of information to the public can be as important as recovering from the incident itself. President is the company spokesperson with the press.

As you're writing your own plan, think about what it feels like to face disruption. When incidents happen, *what* do you do, *when* do you do it, and *who* does it? Think of your plan as a complete chronological checklist, moving step by step so everyone feels empowered to help. Once the situation is under control, the final step of your plan should be identifying how to prevent/handle these impacts in the future.

Let the fear of close calls and possible total loss motivate you to steer clear of repeating the same mistakes and prepare you for the next, different challenge. Conduct a postmortem on the disruption event. In hindsight, what happened? What was the event, how did it first appear, then unfold and morph? How and when did it end? What new path are you on now that the disruption event is over? What were your responses? What did you do right; what did you do wrong; what would you do differently? Did you take certain actions too quickly or too slowly? Is there anything you wish you had done ahead of time? Do it now. This is how you start to create your incident response plan, a "disruption playbook," so you can ensure that the valuable lessons become deeply ingrained.

That said, the incident response plan is one piece of your two-part overall preparedness strategy. When you're satisfied with your plan, it's time to address the other half of becoming collision proof.

Risk Management

Risk management involves ascertaining operational, financial, and regulatory issues and any other areas in which risks might occur. The main emphasis of risk management is that you never need your incident response plan. Yet you can't predict or prevent every risk, which is why these two components go hand in hand.

A big part of risk management is actually risk identification. Simply identifying the risks that would have the largest impact on your organization, career, or life is often harder than managing them. You can't identify every risk, nor should you waste time trying. Identify the ones that are within your control and that are substantive enough to really do some damage. As far as I'm concerned, one injured person is too much risk, especially if it's avoidable. What are your deal breakers? What things are so harmful that they warrant your investment of time, resource training, or other mitigation strategies to prevent them? In each area of your business and life, identify what those risks are.

Here is a good example of a risk assessment and mitigation plan from TUI Group, one of the world's largest and most diversified tourism businesses headquartered in Germany.[15] Like the incident response plan, what to do, when, how, and by whom is codified with no uncertainties. From one glance at this one-pager, company stakeholders can identify which risks are more likely to happen than others and where they stand in relation to them.

---

15   TUI Group. *2019 Annual Report of the TUI Group*. PDF file. December 11, 2019, 46. www.annualreports.com/HostedData/AnnualReports/PDF/LSE_TUI_2019.pdf.

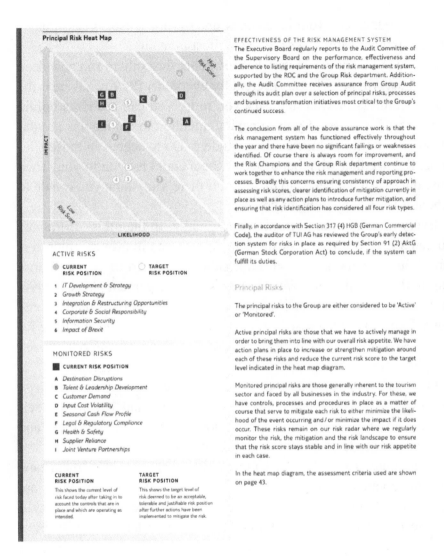

Principal Risk Heat Map

IMPACT

LIKELIHOOD

High Risk Score

Low Risk Score

ACTIVE RISKS

● CURRENT RISK POSITION   ○ TARGET RISK POSITION

1 *IT Development & Strategy*
2 *Growth Strategy*
3 *Integration & Restructuring Opportunities*
4 *Corporate & Social Responsibility*
5 *Information Security*
6 *Impact of Brexit*

MONITORED RISKS

■ CURRENT RISK POSITION

A *Destination Disruptions*
B *Talent & Leadership Development*
C *Customer Demand*
D *Input Cost Volatility*
E *Seasonal Cash Flow Profile*
F *Legal & Regulatory Compliance*
G *Health & Safety*
H *Supplier Reliance*
I *Joint Venture Partnerships*

CURRENT RISK POSITION
This shows the current level of risk faced today after taking in to account the controls that are in place and which are operating as intended.

TARGET RISK POSITION
This shows the target level of risk deemed to be an acceptable, tolerable and justifiable risk position after further actions have been implemented to mitigate the risk.

EFFECTIVENESS OF THE RISK MANAGEMENT SYSTEM
The Executive Board regularly reports to the Audit Committee of the Supervisory Board on the performance, effectiveness and adherence to listing requirements of the risk management system, supported by the ROC and the Group Risk department. Additionally, the Audit Committee receives assurance from Group Audit through its audit plan over a selection of principal risks, processes and business transformation initiatives most critical to the Group's continued success.

The conclusion from all of the above assurance work is that the risk management system has functioned effectively throughout the year and there have been no significant failings or weaknesses identified. Of course there is always room for improvement, and the Risk Champions and the Group Risk department continue to work together to enhance the risk management and reporting processes. Broadly this concerns ensuring consistency of approach in assessing risk scores, clearer identification of mitigation currently in place as well as any action plans to introduce further mitigation, and ensuring that risk identification has considered all four risk types.

Finally, in accordance with Section 317 (4) HGB (German Commercial Code), the auditor of TUI AG has reviewed the Group's early detection system for risks in place as required by Section 91 (2) AktG (German Stock Corporation Act) to conclude, if the system can fulfil its duties.

Principal Risks

The principal risks to the Group are either considered to be 'Active' or 'Monitored'.

Active principal risks are those that we have to actively manage in order to bring them into line with our overall risk appetite. We have action plans in place to increase or strengthen mitigation around each of these risks and reduce the current risk score to the target level indicated in the heat map diagram.

Monitored principal risks are those generally inherent to the tourism sector and faced by all businesses in the industry. For these, we have controls, processes and procedures in place as a matter of course that serve to mitigate each risk to either minimize the likelihood of the event occurring and / or minimize the impact if it does occur. These risks remain on our risk radar where we regularly monitor the risk, the mitigation and the risk landscape to ensure that the risk score stays stable and in line with our risk appetite in each case.

In the heat map diagram, the assessment criteria used are shown on page 43.

Writing Your Risk Management Plan

I highly recommend creating your own principal risk heat map to plot risks from low risk score to high risk score. There are no calculations or formulas here. Simply determine each risk's potential impact on your business, your career, your loved ones, and so forth. Also, "guesstimate" how likely those same risks are to manifest in reality.

How do you know which risks are likelier than others and how deep their impact will be? This is different for everyone. But my advice is the same: regardless of what industry you're in, you can see risks unfold in real time for others if you're paying attention to companies in your industry or similar industries. Be a student. Go to school in those situations. Realize that what happened to them could happen to you. Then figure out *why* it happened to them and if there's anything you can do to prevent it from happening to you.

Every disruption is a learning opportunity. In the midst of trauma, you can see where your risk management can be improved going forward. You see what additional information you need in your response plan for the next incident. We call these risk management plans, not risk elimination plans. That is not practical. There will be risks that become reality. Expecting otherwise is to plan for the unachievable and hope for the impossible. That's why we must get everything we can out of each disruption. Never let an opportunity for learning go to waste.

One such learning opportunity for the cruise industry was the *Costa Concordia*. That ship was grounded, capsized, and sank because it deviated from its intended course for no good reason, struck a rock, and triggered a cascade of disaster and tragedy.

That singular event caused the entire industry to implement new protocols about following courses without deviation. Now, there are notifications to cruise headquarters if a ship deviates from course. To mitigate the chance of something like that ever happening again, a great deal of discretion was taken away from the wheelhouse. An entire industry learned from one captain's mishap. If you're paying attention in your own industry, career, and life, you can learn from others' expensive lessons as well.

The same can be done from a personal perspective. While you won't need as extensive an incident response plan, personal risk management is crucial. Consider what would threaten your home's safety, your physical health, and your legal safety. Include any people who depend on you and what your commitments are to them, and vice versa.

I'll offer one caveat about risk management—it only works as well as your disciplined approach to identifying the many categories and layers of risk that apply to your situation. It's possible to plan for real and likely risks but not those you never could have seen coming. That's when you must rely on your incident response plan.

There's an adage that to win, you have to avoid losing. Active risk mitigation and a solid incident response plan are the best way to ensure you or your company is not so caught up in strategies to succeed that you forget to ask, "Where's the threat?" When the *Empress of the North* grounded, the incident response plan kept us going. The support of first responders and community members was critically important. Build those relationships in advance and follow the plan. And then, do as we did—revise your risk management plan to prevent a similar incident from happening in the future.

CHAPTER 7

Protect Your Value

The Sixth Protocol for Survival, Stability, and Success

The opportunities of man are limited only by his imagination. But so few have imagination that there are ten thousand fiddlers to one composer.

—Charles Kettering

$\mathbf{B}$efore COVID-19, severe acute respiratory syndrome coronavirus (SARS) caused respiratory and flu-like symptoms in its victims in 2002 and 2003. The SARS health crisis came shortly on the heels of 9/11 and the related financial market downturn, a time when the cruise industry had yet to fully recover from the enormous impacts of 2001 and 2002.

I was a senior executive at Holland America Line when the new SARS virus broke out. The Asian market was directly affected as the disease first emerged in China. All global cruise companies had ships in the region. Like so many events, a regional development rapidly becomes a global concern and impact. The entire industry felt the disruption's impact, and we had to reposition ships and adopt new screening and health protocols. As I've said, in the cruise business, any event has the potential of a ripple effect that can become a wave, affecting the whole industry.

We canceled cruises in the hardest-hit areas and redirected others to safer locales. Customers, of course, had their immediate travel plans altered, and they weren't thrilled. That meant more time and energy spent managing their needs and expectations.

We knew we needed to revise and redirect future bookings, but we weren't sure how far out to plan.

A *New York Times* article from early that year detailed some changes we had to make:

> On April 25, the 16 members of the International Council of Cruise Lines adopted a set of guidelines for screening passengers for SARS. Passengers must fill out questionnaires about recent travel, and lines will be expected to deny boarding to guests who have been in those places the council has designated areas of special concern—as of April 28, Hong Kong, mainland China and Singapore—within the previous 10 days.[16]

Some cruises we rerouted permanently. Others we put on hold until further assessment could be made. The entire industry wondered what the near future might look like under the new restrictions and safety procedures. Even after the immediate SARS threat ended (successful containment by quarantining the sick), we needed a long-term strategy to rebuild the public's trust in the safety and convenience of cruising—specifically, the value of the experience.

---

16   Edwin McDowell, "Travel Advisory: Cruises Change Routes Since SARS Outbreak, *New York Times*, May 4, 2003, www.nytimes.com/2003/05/04/travel/travel-advisory-cruises-change-routes-since-sars-outbreak.html.

The Pricing Problem

To fully understand what I'm about to share about value and price, I'd like you to understand the tiered nature of brands, products, and pricing in the cruising industry.

Contemporary cruises have lower ticket prices than premium and luxury cruises. The ships are larger, accommodating more guests, so they earn a significant share of their profits through onboard purchases by guests. Their casinos, bars, shops, shore excursion tours, and exclusive restaurants are usually not covered in the cost of the cruise. This attracts customers looking for an inexpensive initial price. The cruise industry uses the word *contemporary* because *mass market* doesn't accurately reflect the extraordinary value of a cruise vacation, but that's a way to think about the cruise industry tiers. Consider these cruises the Chevy option.

Luxury cruises, on the other hand, referred to as all-inclusive, include these experiences in the initial price so everything is covered up front. And they offer more personalized experiences with higher-quality meals, more dining options, beautiful theaters, and overall grander service. The ships get smaller, the cabins' amenities and service quality increase, and the places they go are more exotic. Customers pay more for all-inclusive service. These cruises are the Mercedes of cruise experiences.

Chevrolet and Mercedes both produce vehicles, but they serve different functions and target different customers. There are high-volume brands with mass market appeal. There are also moderate-volume brands with some premium/luxury additions. Then there are low-volume brands focused entirely on an extraordinary driving and ownership experience. As the quality gets higher, the price goes up. The same goes for almost every industry.

In 2003, Holland America sat somewhere in between as a leading premium brand—more like the Lexus or Cadillac of cruising. We offered many features of luxury cruising with a price tag that appealed to a broader customer base. But the way we operated was closer to luxury, with many touches of luxury included in the initial price.

In the midst of SARS, like previous disruptions, we saw that contemporary brands were able to turn the demand dial quickly through steep discounting and shorter, close-to home itineraries. They were structured for volume. They made it work by leveraging onboard upsells. Customers booked for the low initial price and then splurged on extras during the cruise.

Price adjustments proved more complicated for premium and luxury cruises, however, and that included us. We had less leeway in our pricing because the high-quality amenities we offered cost us more. We operated with 30 percent fewer passengers on board a similar-size ship because we provided more space ratio of all types to our guests. Our cabins were larger, and we had more dining options, more social areas, more deck space, and grander spas. What we didn't have was an easy way to generate more sources of onboard revenue during the cruise. We couldn't overcome the impact of discounting the cruise price with increased onboard revenue like our larger competitors.

Still, we had to compete. We couldn't adopt the strategy of the contemporary cruise companies. You can't compare a Chevy to a Lexus. But what could we do to recover?

The cruise industry as a whole had learned from prior disruption events that it was possible to bring people back with severe price discounting. But the length of time that method required to get back to normal pricing levels was too costly for us. Once people got used to the $399 price point, it would take them a while to become comfortable with $799 again. The premium and luxury cruise industry had learned the hard way that we needed to protect our value—not try to price match with other cruise tiers in times of decreased demand. In the 2003 SARS disruption, that meant we had to resist the urge to undermine our pricing and value proposition.

And let me tell you, it's a lot of work *not* to play chicken with competitors and customers when it comes to pricing. But when you overreact by over-discounting in an attempt to get a rapid recovery of demand, you will pay a long-term price. You are, in essence, competing with your future self. Undercutting yourself to get through one disruption or economic slowdown means you're still trying to recover when the next one hits. No matter how you look at it, it's bad news for long-term sustainability. It requires a lot of work and time to reestablish your brand. Customers want to know what they can expect from you. And when you lose their belief in your pricing integrity and value proposition, they will find someone else. Imagine going through an extended disruption event and responding with deep discounts. It's a much steeper climb to get back to your regular price because customers have lowered their expectations.

A good friend of mine likes to point out: "No one will respect your brand, product, or services in the marketplace more than you. Everything you do must demonstrate that you take yourself seriously, have exacting standards, and are committed to providing the highest quality and value."

You know this disruption is going to end. The market is going to recover. If you hold on, even when it feels hard, it will pay off in the end. You must find the courage and the fortitude to go through the disruption without adding deadweight you'll have to pull behind you through a market recovery. That's what happens when you ruin your pricing integrity. After the disruption, you have to repair all that pricing damage instead of benefiting from the improved market. Imagine needing three years to restore your pricing. It prevents you from being able to recover the way you should.

Too many company leaders forget that customers are not a static entity. Customers are very smart. Once they realize they can wait for prices to drop or for the next big promotion, they'll just wait. The effect snowballs, so it's hard to turn around. When you drop your price steeply and frequently, customers come to expect ongoing deals and special pricing. They no longer see the value you offer; they become worried about overpaying by not waiting for the next rock-bottom deal. When your customers trust you, your product, or your service, there's a high value in maintaining pricing integrity—even during disruption.

When I first started in the cruise industry, most luxury companies operated with very stable pricing structures, especially the more boutique luxury and premium brands. Over time, I saw a lot of the smaller and midsize cruise companies adopt pricing practices of the much larger, volume-focused cruise companies. Specifically, the cruise industry discovered the revenue management practices of the airline and hotel industries, which also have highly perishable inventory. It is an approach that is dramatically different, and if you get it wrong, the impact on your financial results cannot be recovered for at least two years.

Many got it wrong. I knew that wasn't Holland America's path forward. We had to come up with a pricing and promotion strategy that didn't destroy our customers' value perceptions and their confidence in booking early at prices that reflected our quality of product and experience. We needed to go in the other direction. We needed to focus on protecting our value rather than manipulating demand curves with constant near real-time pricing adjustments. We just weren't big enough at the time, and our price points weren't low enough to play this volume pricing game of cat and mouse with the marketplace.

Protect Your Value

Pricing is both an art and a science. If you throw your company's principles out the door and replace them with steep discounting when a disruption happens, you look desperate. By staying the course with a measured and value-added mentality, you'll be more likely to navigate to full recovery sooner.

At Holland America, we knew protecting our value was crucial to our future success. That meant we were willing to make bold decisions— like choosing to run at less than 100 percent occupancy instead of deeply discounting the empty cabins. In a premium line, it's not worth it to run at 100 percent capacity and make 30 percent less in pricing anyway. The math doesn't work. Better to stay closer to our normal pricing at 80 percent capacity. That was one benefit the premium and luxury tier had over the contemporary brands. Contemporary cruises, however, to recoup their costs, needed every single guest, and then some, on board.

Instead of dropping prices, we started looking at ways to enhance the customer's perception of our value. Free airfare was a good value-add that helped encourage customers to book. That way, the customer was still booking at the regular price but incentivized by a free round-trip plane ticket perceived to be worth hundreds of dollars in added value. By working out volume deals with airlines, we lowered our cost of providing this highly perceived value incentive.

We identified other value-adds that customers loved, like offering an upgrade in the cabin category. Instead of price discounting, we increased the perception of value with small bonuses that didn't cost us much to implement. In some cases, we repositioned our ships to pursue new segments of business. Or we focused on higher closing rates for sales. Or we intercepted our competitors' demand with creative unpublished price-match promotions.

Not all businesses are in a place to use this exact business model. Depending on the company, the disruption, and the resources available, protecting your value takes on a variety of forms. Never during my career did I have the benefit of running a high-volume brand where I could just turn the price dial and voilà—problem solved. I always had to do the hard work and figure out how to dig the business out of the storm.

If All Else Fails, Cover Up

After SARS, Holland America really learned to find creative ways to protect its value. When we stopped trying to compete with other cruise-line tiers and instead emphasized the completely unique premium experiences we were offering, the value-add strategies enabled Holland America to recover in sync with the market. We didn't have to repair any damage done to our pricing integrity because we didn't over-discount. We were also in a position to launch the incredibly successful "Signature of Excellence" initiative, which set us on a course of financial recovery and growth that was exceptionally positive.

The last thing we wanted to do was overreact and make decisions that would make the disruption last longer for us than it did for anyone else. We didn't want to remain in the past after the disruption had passed. I've got another personal story that illustrates this principle.

I spent a lot of time with my grandfather in my youth because of my disrupted family situation. He was a sustenance hunter and fishermen. So in my time with him, I worked untold hours helping hunt, pack meat out of the bush, and fish.

My grandfather was also a wildcatter in Montana, a bronc buster (he was accomplished at the rodeo), and a Golden Gloves boxer. He was a tough guy to the core, and he used to tell me,

> If you ever have somebody coming at you and attacking you, especially someone bigger than you, you don't fight. You cover up, you move, then you cover up again. You let them punch themselves out. Pretty soon that guy will get slower. He'll be huffing and puffing. And that's when you do your work.

His advice has always stuck in my mind and for more than just protecting myself. When you're in a bad situation, either you or your company is taking blows in one form or another. But if you blow all your energy, your finances, and your value while fighting something that's bigger than you, you're fighting a losing battle.

There's a better way to come out of the fight. Protect your value, then move when you can. Once the storm blows over, you can recover more quickly if you haven't lost your value. By maintaining your prices, you maintain your integrity. As long as your customers still know who you are, they know they can count on you. Then, boom, they're back to where they were before the event, and your company recovers. Protecting your value is one of the keys to coming through intact.

Increase Your Value by Lightening Your Load

Let's talk about shedding deadweight.

The cruise industry made it through SARS and went on to navigate a dozen other major disruptions. But COVID-19 has simply been the biggest event of our industry—the biggest disruption of all our lifetimes, really, in all aspects of our businesses, careers, and personal lives.

A cruise line may look like a tangible, solid fleet of ships with specific destinations. In reality, those assets are as fluid as the oceans and seas on which they operate. Just like a locomotive, the newer, most preferred, efficient, and financially successful ships are the engines that pull along the older vessels in the fleet. Older vessels are less attractive, especially to new and younger cruise customers, and more expensive to maintain and operate. It's like pulling a deadweight behind you that inhibits your speed and performance. Cruise lines are always looking for ways to jettison this older tonnage without taking a negative hit to their balance sheets.

Meanwhile, what you don't see is that just on the horizon are amazing new ships—some under construction, some contracted several years into the future. There are billions of dollars of new builds that reflect the vision of what cruising will look like in the future with improved technologies and higher profit margins. These are the equivalent of footprints in the future.

COVID-19 has accelerated the need to get to the future represented by those new ships more quickly and to operate in that future more profitably. At the time of COVID, there were 278 ships operating with over 500,000 total berths capacity, plus 72 new builds under construction or on order with 244,000 berths additional capacity at an estimated cost of $58 billion. During the pause, the major cruise lines have not been treading water—they've been selling, mothballing, or scrapping older ships at an unprecedented rate to make way for a new future.

What deadweight are you pulling behind your business, your career, or your life into a future that requires a leaner, more agile profile? What are your new builds that are pulling you forward—through COVID and into the future?

Lighten your load, and you'll free up energy to focus on your real, intrinsic value.

The Intrinsic Value Equation

Protecting your pricing integrity and your value perception (how customers perceive your value) is critical—especially when rebuilding in an industry with fragile economics. You don't want to damage your long-term value or, more accurately, your value perception. You have to know the unique benefits of what you offer. You have to show people how much they're gaining by investing in your value. Thus, the notion of value must have an expanded meaning: sensible, sustainable, durable, ethical, authentic, social, and green.

I wrote an article for a sea trade publication in which I talked about pricing integrity. I built this equation for that article so cruise companies could calculate their intrinsic value. We can all understand customers better if we consider our operations based on this equation. So, what exactly is intrinsic value? I think of it in the cruise and travel business as "experience value." What is the core experience and value of dreams come true? Expectations met and exceeded? Lifetime memories? New-found friends around the world? Discovery? Lifelong learning? I think deeply about those types of experiential attributes that touch the hearts and souls of travelers. I work hard with teams of passionate, creative communicators to make those core intrinsic experience values as tangible in the minds of consumers as possible and as unique and proprietary to my company as possible. Done well, those experiential elements are worth the price alone. Only then do I start adding on all the other even more tangible components of value—the places and ports of call, the ship itself, the comfort and amenities of the staterooms, the private verandas, the amazing levels of genuine service and hospitality provided by officers and crew members, the culinary program, entertainment, enrichment programs such as informative lectures and learning opportunities, and more.

You get the point. Value arguments are additive: how much more experience and tangibles you are getting for your time and expenditure. Pricing arguments, on the other hand, are most often reductionist in approach—focused on discounts, savings, and special time-sensitive promotions. Two different approaches for sure. In the cruise business, with high fixed operating costs, especially for the premium and luxury segments of the industry, you cannot discount your way to profitability. You'd better know how to position and communicate the value of the experience you are offering.

The Intrinsic Value Equation

$$(IV) = \frac{X + Y + Z}{X \times Y}$$

(IV) is Intrinsic Value

Above the division lign, X, Y, and Z are your business variables—your biggest sources of value. They're what you offer with what you sell. For cruise lines, this could include the ship, itinerary, expedition team, and enrichment program. Look at the variables specific to your industry. All these make up the core value of what you're offering.

All this value you're offering is divided by the consumer in time and multiplied by money. This explains the division sign and the multiplication sign of the equation. At the bottom of the fraction is the financial cost to the customer (X) multiplied by the time investment they're making (Y).

After all, your customer is taking a risk. They could waste time and money. They're not just out the cash if that ten-day trip isn't worth it. They lose the time spent choosing and planning the trip, anticipating the trip, and the actual ten days of the trip. Then they'll feel underwhelmed for months or years to come. It's not just money. It's time, energy, and dreams. You must have empathy for the customer on the buying side of the equation.

That's one thing this equation gives you. It puts you in your customer's shoes. It's important to remember that every customer is calculating your cost and value in their head. Every time your customer makes a purchase decision, they have to make peace with the cost of the value. We all do this when we spend money, whether knowingly or not. We look at what we know about the product and our own experience as shoppers. Everybody has different variables that matter to them, but one way or another, we're all calculating price and value.

As a business owner, company executive, or professional, how can we help customers know what they're getting in return? You can help shape their calculations by defining the unique value you bring to the table. It's really critical to emphasize *exactly* what it is you offer. When you think like a customer, you can pinpoint your most important variables and emphasize them when communicating your value. Personalization goes a long way toward protecting price integrity and value perception. Carefully craft each piece of your content, communications, and touchpoints to emphasize your value. Detail is essential. These become the variables that the customer adds up to determine your worth.

So how does this equation really work? How does X plus Y plus Z, divided by time and multiplied by money, give your offer more perceived value than your competition? To answer that, I'm going to give you another example.

As a senior executive leading some of the world's greatest boutique and premium cruise lines, I reminded customers of all the variables we included in their ticket price. I didn't want our customers to only think of the ship and the destinations. When a customer is in the middle of a purchase decision and I'm fighting hard to support an extraordinary price, I highlight the key attributes being offered. These include safety, comfort, special design features, new expeditions, and other unique, cutting-edge elements. Each individual variable is a reason for the customer to be on this unique ship and justifies why the experience costs more.

And it does. As an example, in some cases, our small-ship cruises cost three times as much as a normal Alaska cruise. Every unique aspect of the product comes into the equation and adds to the premium, unusual experience that customers can expect. Of course they'd pay more for such incredible value. They can compare our prices to our competitors', but we addressed that part of the equation too. On a typical seven-day Alaska cruise, you go to the four same ports everybody else goes to, sometimes with five ships in port at once. So you might have ten thousand or more tourists packed into a tiny little Alaskan town at the same time, doing the same artificially created mass market tours. That's not comparable at all to the experience I'm committed to providing customers.

A big part of our intrinsic value is what happens both on board our ships and throughout the trip. Guests get the freshest local culinary experiences. We take them deep into the destination experience and serve craft beers and wine, gourmet seafood, and fresh produce, all the very finest elements to enhance the experience. We offer adventurous tours in float planes, helicopters, zodiacs, and kayaks. When customers have finished the adventure and are ready for some alone time, every cabin has a private balcony where they can experience the fresh air and vistas of Alaska, anytime they want. They can stand out over the edge of the ship and see the scenery or relax in front of a great big wide-screen TV with multiple channels. They can head to the gym, spa, or various lounges; take in a live nature lecture; or find a quiet corner on deck to marvel at the stars, shoreline, and rugged wilderness surrounding them.

One of my favorite ships has a platform high up on each side of the bow that fans out and can be suspended above nature. If there are porpoises or whales chasing the bow or when the ship is nudging its way through ice up to the face of a glacier, guests get to stand suspended in air right over the top of it all. It's an unbelievable feeling, and most people are excited to be closer to nature than they ever imagined. Imagine sailing into remote coves with the entire vessel shut down and made silent in order for guests to fully appreciate the serenity and majesty of nature, like you might experience on a private yacht anchoring in a cove for the evening. You can see fish jumping, you can hear loons calling, and sometimes there's a moose or bear wandering the shoreline.

Most people never get to have that kind of experience in Alaska. But they do when I design a product. What's that worth? It's the extras that make it a high-value experience. It's about more than just the ship and destination. It's for those who want more—much more—out of their travel experiences. Before a person becomes aware of small-ship cruising, or even interested in what it might have to offer them, they've most likely taken several large-ship cruises. They know what cruising is. They know the advantages of cruising. You're not selling them on cruising itself but on the added value of deeper, highly personal, and meaningful experiences, made possible by the unique attributes of the ship, itinerary, crew, and fellow like-minded passengers.

The average cost of contemporary cruise lines in 2020 was $200 a day per person. Regular cruise travelers will know that a couple spends $400 a day or $3,000 per week, and they're used to that price. But eventually they hear people talk. They see extraordinary pictures of smaller cruise ships going through the heart of Europe with only 180 people on board. They see pictures of ships going into Antarctica with only 100 passionate nature lovers. Smaller ships make that intimate experience possible, but now the price is $1,000 a day. That's very expensive to the average cruise traveler. And the cabins are smaller and different from what they're used to.

But it's not about the ships. It's about the experiences. A savvy luxury river-cruise company will communicate the value of the experience and the unique attributes of each location they travel to. Each stop along the itinerary is a once-in-a-lifetime experience. Each moment is unforgettable.

When I consult with companies, I'm not talking about how to salvage 2021. I get paid to create exciting energy that pulls companies into success in 2022 and 2023. I spend a tremendous amount of time making sure I'm completely up to date with everything at their company. Then I highlight what I see as the important issues, and we work together to define their intrinsic value. I help them discover that value and reestablish growth and profitability. Often companies are wasting a lot of time and resources to pursue an unrealistic picture of 2021. By looking ahead to 2022 and 2023 instead, they can improve the odds and the speed at which they'll stand apart from the competition and achieve growth.

I charge more than other people because I deliver more. I do my homework and differentiate my approach based on specific client needs. In so doing, I make the perception of my value tangible. When it's tangible, people can make a comfortable decision. Of course I cost more, but I'm the guy they want.

Part of intrinsic value is seeing the value in yourself. Don't stay small and focused on setbacks or limitations when you could instead gain millions in revenue by communicating your value. When you redefine your value per the intrinsic value equation, you can see the strategies that will land you the customers you need.

Using this equation in a personal setting works much the same way. You will still have variables to add up that will differ depending on your situation. Focus on the value of what you can do. What are the variables that will propel you into 2022, 2023, and beyond? Identify that value and protect it at all costs.

Finding and Expressing Your Intrinsic Value: The One Best Thing You Have

Part of my job is helping travel companies and their travel agents understand how to increase their value by focusing on what they excel at offering. Your intrinsic value should never be compromised.

Intrinsic value is a shift in thinking—from hardware to software, from features to benefits. You're focusing on the core value of your one-of-a-kind experience. Your customer's perception of your value is what matters most. You have to communicate with depth, detail, and passion in order to express the intrinsic value of a boutique experience or a specialty product. It doesn't matter what kind of company you have. You always want to emphasize your value.

I remember seeing a flyer for a company that installed roofing gutters. Talk about a less-than-exciting product. But this flyer was unbelievable.

It deeply expressed the benefits of their product by describing the home-owner experience of never having to clean your gutters again. "When leaves and pine needles get stuck in gutters, it causes a mess of water around your foundation." Every line hit you with the value these gutters would provide. It made you want to get new gutters from this company because they clearly understood your needs. That flyer expressed the whole essence of intrinsic value.

If you're a freelancer in art or writing, you could just say, "My price is one hundred and twenty dollars per hour." Or you could describe the personal experience of what you offer and the needs you serve, establishing your unique value. To do that, you need to know your customers and their needs. This is a crucial mindset for someone who wants to serve their customers with integrity and value. As a company, listen to your customers' feedback. Take what your customers tell you and infuse it with your own experiences, perspectives, and dreams.

The secret to intrinsic value is to learn what customers want, provide it, and then demonstrate that you're providing it. Most companies at least try to express the intrinsic value of what they offer. The most successful companies really get into their customers' shoes and examine what they want. And the best companies master the ability to communicate that value in a way their customers will understand.

That's why you've seen some car dealerships turn buying a car into an "experience." Range Rover's intrinsic value, for example, is designed more around the experience of owning the car than it is around the car's features. The same is true of Jeep and Lexus. Earlier in this chapter, I mentioned Cadillac as a premium luxury example, and I didn't even have to explain why. The public understands its intrinsic value.

Every company has an opportunity to build that same perception of value based on customer experience. This becomes even more important during a disruption. The first customers to spend big money coming out of a downturn are typically the better-off consumers looking for real value over cheap bargains. The more sophisticated seller is the one who proves that they're the one offering the best value.

When both you and your customers understand the value you offer, the customers stop looking to cut a deal. They're less likely to argue over a $500 dealer markup. They stop waiting for a discount. They become eager to buy because they want to be part of the experience you're selling.

Of course, this means you have to provide genuine value to your customers. When you market your product based on that value, you can use your proceeds to enhance your value even more. You get to stop spending money where it's not doing you or your customers any good. You also free up resources to provide your customers even better experiences. This creates a virtuous cycle of progress.

If there is anything you want while you're in the fog, it's progress.

Your Personal Value

Many colleagues and past clients have reached out to me lately because COVID disrupted their careers. They ask me what they can do to find their way through the fog. I tell them to use this time to add value to what they offer. They might have been furloughed, had their time cut back to half, or been let go entirely. But if they're committed to improving their value, innovating and communicating that to customers, there are a tremendous number of opportunities available.

One of the best opportunities you can seize right now is taking an online course. Now is the time for independent study. So many people are just sitting back and complaining, not realizing they have control over their future. If you're furloughed, let your employer know that you understand this cutback was necessary. Then let them know you're committed to growing, and you're using this time to add to your skill set and increase your value so that when you come back into the company, you're ready for the new market. You can be self-defeating, or you can be proactive and value creating.

Like the rest of this book, this isn't just business advice. Intrinsic value applies to your personal life too. Consider your personal elements—perhaps dependability, experience, or a special skill. Just as pricing integrity can be difficult to reestablish, personal integrity works the same way. Your family and friends will remember if you become unreliable when you're lost in the fog together. What if you let yourself go when they need you most? What if their perception of you as a person that they can count on changes forever? I've had a lot of Zoom calls with people during the COVID downturn, and I've been shocked at how lackadaisical some folks let themselves become in professional discussions with me. Some of them have just plain given up. That's a terrible look and inspires no confidence in the people around you.

How you show up personally and professionally adds value to your offer. The future of all work is results based, and integrity solidifies confidence in those results. Being raised by a single father who built an extraordinary company around Alaskan tourism and small-ship cruising helped teach me that you have to stick to your values, no matter what you face.

That lesson in value has helped me navigate through the fog.

Every fog.

Now it's your turn.

CHAPTER 8

Outlasting the Fog

For a man to conquer himself is the first and noblest of all victories.

—Plato

I n the winter of 1968, when I was eleven years old, my grandfather and I traveled by a combined passenger and cargo jet to Yakutat, a remote town on Alaska's wild coastline near the massive Hubbard Glacier. We arrived during a raging winter storm with extremely high winds, freezing temperatures, and plenty of new snow. From there, we traveled by bush plane thirty miles into the remote wilderness. This was my grandfather's favorite location for his annual moose hunt. I always joined him to help with the hard work of packing the game out of the forest.

From the plane, I sighted brown bears and moose and observed an enormous wolf loping along the high ridgelines. I couldn't believe the size of those bears—large as a pickup truck—or how fast that wolf moved across the frozen ridges. The blizzard let up, but the far-below-freezing temperatures and bone-chilling winds remained.

We landed on a short dirt patch near the Dangerous River (yes, that's the real name of this large glacial river), unloaded our hunting gear, and waved goodbye to the pilot. Our journey ended at a rustic forest service cabin perched above the riverbank. There was no form of long-distance communication and no other people for miles. Our only way of communicating in an emergency was to plant a red flag at the end of the snow-covered dirt runway and wait. Bush pilots knew to look for those flags as a signal for help as they flew across the area.

Once we settled into the small four-bunk cabin and got a fire going in the woodburning stove, I wanted to explore the area and look for signs of moose and other wildlife. My grandfather reminded me to take my rifle for safety. I had a bolt-action Winchester .300 Magnum rifle with a powerful Zeiss scope, and I'd been trained to use it. We had an emergency plan in place for if or when we got separated (as in the fifth protocol). I was to fire three shots into the air if I ran into any trouble. He would fire one shot in return, and we would each continue to fire one shot alternating between us until we were able to locate one another.

As I entered the thick forest, bushwhacking through Alaska's famously difficult alder bush, I found a game trail and started to follow it. I heard bears growling ahead and decided to give that area a wide berth. We had lost a moose to a big brown bear in this area a year earlier, and I knew they were dangerous. I was so intent on avoiding the bears that soon I was no longer sure of the way back to the cabin. I did know that I could head east to the river and travel downriver to the campsite. The location of the midday sun told me to angle left through the woods to find the riverbank.

When I eventually broke out of the thick alder bushes just above the river, I heard a rustling nearby. I turned to see an enormous porcupine eating bark off the bushes. It must have weighed at least thirty pounds, and its wrapping of quills was amazing. I decided my best shot at safety was to scramble down the bank to walk along the riverbed.

The riverbed was muddy but manageable—for a while. Then suddenly, the ground fell out from under me. I sank down into the earth before I understood what was happening. Quicksand. The silt runoff from the river combined with the water below had created a dangerous trap under what appeared to be a solid surface. The quicksand was up to my chest. The harder I fought to move toward an edge, the more stuck I became. Then the edges collapsed, widening the hole I was in. There was no way out.

I fired the first of three shots, a booming crack in the silence of the vast wilderness—and my gun jammed. I could not eject the spent shell to chamber a second shot, much less a third. The spent shell had expanded, perhaps due to the temperature extremes, or perhaps it was a defective casing. I was in real trouble.

My grandpa must have heard the one shot because a few seconds later, I heard him fire off an answering shot. But I couldn't respond.

I looked around, desperate. There was one lone alder bush just beyond my reach. It offered the only chance to stop the suction of mud surrounding and trapping my body. That's when I realized there was another use for my rifle. By turning it around, holding it by the barrel, and reaching out, I hoped to be able to loop the rifle's shoulder strap around a thick branch of the alder.

This gave me a chance to settle my thoughts and calm my breathing. I got the strap looped over a branch and pulled with all my strength. Inch by inch, I squirmed my body up and out of the hole.

I lay on the ground, exhausted, soaked, and freezing, with my teeth chattering. Then I climbed back up to the tree line and followed the river back toward camp. When I emerged through the trees, my grandfather was watching for me. He saw that I was in bad shape and rushed me inside. I got out of my wet clothes, warmed by the fire, and drank black coffee with bourbon. We both agreed I'd definitely used one of my seven lives that day. We also agreed not to mention the incident to my father.

I learned firsthand that day about controlling my thoughts, emotions, and reactions in an emergency. Many times in my career and my life, people have commented on my quiet calm in the midst of a raging storm of disruption. I call this my endurance mindset. It's a skill that has served me well, and I first began mastering it in the quicksand of '68.

Remaining calm in the storm requires an endurance mindset. This is an important skill you need to get through the unexpected. Let's look at how to build this calm mindset—without the quicksand.

Building an Endurance Mindset

You may remember me mentioning that I've trained for and completed several Ironman events. Ironman is the top endurance event in the world, with long-distance endurance races in three different sports combined into one. It begins with a 2.4-mile open-water swim, followed by a 112-mile bike course, and finishes with a full 26.2-mile marathon. Competitors have up to seventeen hours to complete the whole race, which begins before dawn and often ends in the dark.

The swim generally begins with two thousand or more athletes—a literal sea of humans moving from land to water. Not just moving, but actually kicking, stroking, jostling, breathing, sighting. Many athletes in that seething mass of people begin to feel anxious and a sense of panic until things sort themselves out after the first few hundred yards. Sometimes the shock of cold water and the physical nature of the swim start causes some to pull up, tread water, and regroup. It is challenging for sure. If you are to have a heart attack and die in an Ironman event, it is by far most likely to happen during the swim start.

No matter how much you prepare, your heart and adrenaline still crank into overdrive. In that moment, in that chaos, only one piece of knowledge helped me endure: I knew I had done the training, and I knew I was ready. I reminded myself of this repeatedly to stay calm throughout the swim. Because of my endurance mindset, I was able to use the adrenaline to my advantage.

I've now done three full Ironman events, nearly a dozen half-Ironman events, and numerous other endurance race events—duathlons, trail races, and challenging bike events, including the grueling bike climb up Haleakala on Maui. The endurance mindset needed for Ironman is a different game from that of other races. You can't show up at that starting line and just do your best. You have to know that you've done the work and you're prepared with proper strategy, or you're not going to stay the course. Training for these events makes you stronger, more capable, and more confident. When I show up at that starting line in the dark morning hours, I'm not just physically ready, I'm mentally and emotionally ready. All are equally important.

The endurance mindset will benefit you in all aspects of life. The process I used for the Ironman can be used by anyone to prepare for the disruptions in their life with mental strength and fortitude. First, to really succeed at something, you have to know you've done the work to get there and that the accomplishment is more than worth it.

Do the Work

Training or preparing—that's doing the work—makes you both capable and confident. It also makes you stronger for the next challenge. When I show up at the next endurance race event or the next industry disruption, no matter what it is, I know I'm ready because I've done the work.

When you're in the midst of a business disruption, your preparation is what keeps you in the endurance mindset. If you're seeing other companies pivoting and adjusting course successfully, you're not going to panic. You know you'll find your way through. The same thing happens when you're looking for a new career, and you see others getting incredible jobs while you're still searching. You don't have to worry that you're doing something wrong. Doing the work allows you to know your strengths, accept your limitations, and run your own race in any form of competition. Patience, focus, and consistency will get you there.

So how do you know what work needs to be done? You're nearly finished with this book, so a large portion of your work is complete. The six protocols we've gone through in this book are the tools you can use to keep training.

Following the six protocols during a disruption proves to yourself, your company, and your partners that you've done the work and can handle the issue. The beautiful thing about disruption is it's an ongoing cycle of strength. The six protocols prepare you for disruption, but there will always be another one. With each passing storm, you'll be even more prepared for the next. You'll build the confidence to know that you can endure. And, more importantly, you'll know that you can also handle the mental and emotional impact of the disruption.

After all, in the same way you physically prepare, you also need to put time and effort into the endurance mindset spiritually, emotionally, and mentally. Always move beyond simple survival. You don't finish the Ironman by just trying to survive. You have to *know* you will survive and immediately move into the actions needed for stability and success. It's a shift of focus from recovery to growth, which is possible through your flexibility, the work you put into protecting your value, your preparation for new challenges, and your confidence from your practice. Get your mind to align with your objectives and train your mind to tolerate discomfort. In this way, you will always be prepared.

Training means both understanding what's required of you and strengthening your preparedness. You don't train for the Ironman by running the entire Ironman every day. Instead, you trust the cumulative effect of your training across swimming, biking, and running that meld together into your overall preparation. An endurance mindset lets you push through, even if you encounter a surprisingly harsh reality.

I expected my first Ironman to be hard, and I trained hard to match my expectations. Of course, I had no idea how hard it would really be. A lot of disruption events are like that. Even when you think you're ready for anything, something can happen that you had no idea was even possible. You feel exhausted, distressed, and frustrated. At that point, you can quiet all that noise by engaging a mindset that refuses to stop.

The protocols in this book enable you to train for different aspects of disruption, just like I trained for each of the three Ironman events separately. The goal is for you to practice implementing all of them together seamlessly, even when you're *not* in a disruption, so you're used to flipping between them. Then, when you're in the midst of disruption, you can call on each of the protocols when needed and use them to propel you out of the fog. The more you practice, the more quickly you can stabilize to find success in any disruption.

Let's take a look at the protocols again.

The 6 Protocols for Survival, Stability, and Success

- Protocol 1—Know Your Waypoint
- Protocol 2—Stay Afloat
- Protocol 3—Find Your First First
- Protocol 4—Get Flexible
- Protocol 5—Become Collision Proof
- Protocol 6—Protect Your Value

Every day is a training opportunity. Build your endurance, speed, agility, flexibility, and mental strength with specificity. Train for a cumulative effect.

When you've done all this preparation and a disruption strikes, you can find your way to a new normal more easily because you're already proactively driving results rather than reacting to developments. The cruise industry was proactive as a powerful player in the tourism industry. Then came the great COVID pause of 2020. It will take three or four years to recover, and recovery will require forward momentum. No matter what, you have to believe you'll get there. That faith requires both the choice to believe you'll succeed and the willpower to make it happen.

Combine your willpower with your practice implementing the six protocols, and you'll find the forward momentum that builds perpetual positive energy—perpetual motion. Once you're in motion, it requires less energy to keep going than it does to stop and start again. Think about the six protocols as a means of self-sustaining, renewable energy. The work you do now, before the disruption, is what will propel you to stability and renewed growth.

Manage Your State

Over the course of the Ironman race, it's critically important that participants monitor their overall state. If you're capable of completing an entire element of the race, you may know you have the ability to go hard at that particular discipline. You've proven it to yourself. There are a lot of people who could take any one part of that multisport endurance race and really crush it.

But if you want to finish the event, you must resist the urge to swim as fast, pedal as strong, or run as hard as possible. You have to conserve your energy and set yourself up for success at each stage. If you burn your energy reserves right out of the gate, you'll blow the rest of the event. It's critically important to manage your state beyond the first 2.4 miles of that opening swim. You must know your limits because you have to play the long game.

The same is true in business and in life. Most disruption events are not a sprint but a long course—just like the Ironman. In fact, the Ironman is described as "an endurance racing long-course event." Disruptive events are the same. They require planning and preparing for the long term.

The temptation to push faster is ever present. But if you try to outrun your own preparation, you'll be burned out when the next level of impact comes. Master the endurance mindset, and you'll still be here when the finish line approaches. There will always be people faster than you and slower than you. Remember, you're running your own race. Accept your limitations and know your strengths.

My first Ironman was brutal. That was the first time I'd done 140.6 miles in a competition. In that last leg, even though I thought I'd been pacing myself, I was utterly exhausted, like my body could not go any farther. It was done. There was no magic that could make my legs feel lighter than lead.

That's the point at which the mind takes over the race. Your mind plays as large a role as your physical capabilities. When the body says no, the mind says yes and pulls out hidden reserves the body doesn't even know it has left. My mind knew I had to finish. I had to quiet the noise, seek the finish line, and refuse to stop. My mind took over the race because I'd prepared both physically and mentally. I'd trained my body to maximize what it could do and trained my mind for what my body wasn't capable of.

When you manage your whole state properly, your mind is always prepared. The mind is obviously in the race the whole way, but in the darkest hours, the mind dominates. Just when you *must* give up because you can go no farther, the endurance mindset will take over.

Like the Ironman, disruption requires you to implement all your training simultaneously. You must stay alert and apply the protocols appropriately within the context of the conditions of your situation while monitoring your physical and mental state. In the Ironman bike portion, you must adjust your cornering and hill descent strategy on wet, slick pavement. Tough conditions may require seven hours to finish that portion, not six hours. Accept it and adjust your expectations accordingly. That's an extra hour of hard work, but it will get you through the race in one piece.

And if you don't refuel, you fail.

Refuel Yourself

Part of training is acknowledging the need to refuel, whether personally, professionally, or corporately. What do you need to do your best work? What makes your work more efficient? What calms your mind and strengthens your body to keep you going even in the most demanding circumstances? The trend of self-care may come and go, but it's very true that if you don't refuel your mind, body, and spirit, you won't be doing your best—and you possibly won't make it through the disruption.

In the Ironman, self-care includes proper nutrition, hydration, and a full good night's sleep every day. This keeps your muscles moving, prevents cramps, and tops off your energy for the tasks ahead. In business, self-care might mean making sure you have your key positions filled, learning to stay flexible in working with others, and strengthening what matters most in your organization. Personally, it could mean getting enough sleep and exercise; eating healthy, balanced meals; meditating; and spending quality time with loved ones.

Course conditions change rapidly. You never know what's coming next. When you're properly refueled, you can keep your wits about you and adapt to each new development. Refueling is about preparing for change and staying energized so you're able to adjust your approach as necessary. Refueling is the self-care that replenishes the huge expenditure of energy required to keep going.

You must stay relentlessly committed to the finish line. You're not in this race to finish at record speed. You're in it to cross that finish line. Then you're back in calm waters with sunny skies—until the next storm. You need to keep your wits about you so that you can survive whatever is thrown your way.

Be a Finisher

In baseball, the finisher is the pitcher who enters the diamond in the final inning—when everyone is getting tired. If they're successful, this pitcher finishes (and helps win) the game.

In the last few miles of the Ironman, I'm always running on pure willpower. But I'm confident I can make it there because I've done the training to finish the race. Participants who complete an Ironman event are also called finishers.

The person you become when you're in the thick of the fog reveals your ability (or lack thereof) to stay calm in the storm. When you can stay calm instead of giving into overwhelm, you become the person other people depend on when they get overwhelmed. You're the finisher.

I've earned medals, ribbons, and lanyards with "finisher" written on them from Ironman events in Hawaii, Arizona, Wisconsin, Texas, Utah, Napa Valley, and more. In some endurance events I've been a top ten finisher and even a podium finisher in my age group. What's really amazing about this sport is that once you complete all three disciplines of the race, you can do all kinds of other races too. And they're a lot easier! I can do hundred-mile bike races, half marathons and full marathons, endurance swims, and duathlon racing events. Once you have trained for one, you can succeed in many.

If you train for and survive a big disruption (and remember, you *know* you can survive), you can thrive through many other storms that hit you. Even though each protocol targets a precise area, and even though it might not apply perfectly to your next disruption, the training that the protocols provide makes you stronger and more capable through a wide range of events. Then when something unforeseen happens, you're ready for it—even if you've never imagined the scenario.

That's what happened on the moose hunt with my grandfather. We had gone through our protocols, and we had safety features in place. But when my gun jammed, I had to improvise. Because of my training, I stayed calm in the storm and found a way through it. I had already decided I wasn't going to let the situation get the best of me. I was a finisher when it mattered most.

Being a finisher and having this endurance mindset allows you to be at peace with whatever you're facing. When you find the calm in the midst of the storm, you become the calm for others. And that's the most desirable result of all.

Become One with Disruption

Some who experience disruption let it and its consequences define them forever while others leverage the disruption for their benefit. What you learn during disruption can propel you into a wonderful new future you otherwise would not have experienced had two things not occurred: the disruption and your response to it.

There are some storms you can't fight off, which is why you must become one with them. The disruption is most often beyond your control, so instead of trying to control it, decide to become one with it.

Your response comes from your training, which is following the protocols, starting right now.

If you can ride out the storm no matter what, you're going to reach a place where your ship becomes the sea. Where you become one with that very storm that was tossing you about. The storm is no longer something you're just trying to survive. Now it's a growth experience, and when it passes, you sail off to new horizons.

When I face any disruption, I remember the last lines of the poem I wrote, "The Ship of My Soul":

> My ship becomes the sea
> I steer a new course
> To horizons once beyond my imagining.

Prior to the storm, you didn't have the strength, the skills, or the insights that you gained during the disruption. There are people who stay small and bitter, complaining about what might've been, and then there are people who recover from disruption and become legends.

You can choose to become one with the storm, leverage the disruption, and sail toward success.

Sometimes this seems impossible. But there's always a way. Let me share with you one wild story that has always stuck with me and helps me visualize the ultimate sentiment behind making the best of a disruption.

While sailing on a yacht crossing the Frederick Sound in Southeast Alaska, I spotted a commotion in the water ahead. As I got closer, I observed a pod of killer whales surrounding a sea lion. The adult whales were teaching the younger whales how to hunt. They took turns attacking the sea lion and tossing it into the air. Things looked hopeless for the poor creature.

Suddenly, the sea lion dove beneath the waves and emerged attached to the hull of our yacht, holding itself tight to our ship with one of its giant flippers. I wondered if the whales would endanger the boat, but to my surprise, their sonar could not detect the sea lion. He'd merged himself with our profile and become invisible. The whales milled around but eventually gave up and moved on. The sea lion, still looking terrified but at least calmed down, separated from our boat and hightailed it out of the area.

Remember that sea lion. Instead of fighting against an insurmountable foe, he stopped fighting, got creative, adopted a bigger perspective, and changed the rules. In this case, he used the whales' own strength (sonar ability or echolocation) against them in order to survive. He turned the situation around when it seemed hopeless.

When you feel hopeless, remember the sea lion. And when you find yourself stuck in the fog and blind to your surroundings, remember that staying the course may not be your best option. New dangers could have rolled in your path that you can't see now. Gather new information, take the next best actions, find your waypoint, and make sure you're moving in the best possible direction toward recovery. I think of it as "bail, steer, repair, repeat."

Beacons, like the stars, lighthouses, and buoys, can become shrouded by clouds, darkness, and fog. Those are the times when *you* must become the beacon, for yourself and others. Your values, character, vision, experience, and courage will light the way. Worry and fear do not go away; instead, they are replaced by something else. That something else can only be faith and belief.

Believe in yourself, and others will believe in you. Help others become beacons, and you will have a brighter shared light to apply to each new challenge.

Onward!

Afterword

Beacons of Health: What's Next for the Cruise, Travel, and Tourism Industry in the Post-COVID Era?

The best way to predict your future is to create it.

—Abraham Lincoln

If you work in the cruise, travel, and tourism industry and picked up this book in the 2020s, you probably turned to this chapter first. If you've held a C-level or managerial position in this industry, you already know a little about my work. In the post-COVID years, my perspective on navigating the unprecedented halting of our industry is particularly useful. That said, I intend *Hard Ships* to have a shelf life of at least two decades. At any point in time, you may return to this book, and the six protocols will help you through the fog, be the disruption personal or professional. Yet here in the soaring twenties, you are uniquely concerned with the restart of an industry that had never before ceased operations since its inception in 1907. The novel coronavirus brought a booming industry to a complete halt. We all were left asking, "Now what?" And many leaders of the multitrillion-dollar global travel industry are looking for the same answer.

Much of what you have or will read in *Hard Ships* parallels the advice I gave executives and investors looking to restart post COVID. The best practices and proven strategies I've employed to outlast the last forty-plus years' worth of disruptions have general application.

Anyone enduring change or entering a crisis can use the six protocols. Still, their utility for the cruise industry and beyond after the pandemic cannot be overstated.

I first published the six protocols for survival, stability, and success as the six imperatives for recovery in the leading cruise industry publication *Seatrade Cruise Review*. The observations and advice shared there provided many companies with a road map to make it through the lockdowns, budget deficits, and consumer disinterest in travel. Even though some information is dated, I expect you'll find several nuggets worth your time, so I am sharing that commentary.

Focus on Expedition Cruising

An Updated Look at the Expedition/ Adventure Cruise Market in the COVID-19 Era

May 15, 2020

There's no denying the powerful trends and market forces driving the emergence of expedition cruising as a high-visibility, high-energy category. A quiet, unique corner of the cruise industry suddenly and seemingly was brought to new life—transformed by the cumulative effect of demographics, environmental awareness, a drive for immersive and experiential travel, plus shipbuilding technology, competitive ingenuity, and attraction of financial investments culminating in frequent announcements of new ships; new companies; new experiences, helicopters, and submarines; and new destinations. Indeed, an exciting new chapter for the expedition/adventure cruise business was unfolding rapidly. But today, a somewhat different chapter is being scripted by circumstance. While the specifics of that new chapter remain less than clear, it is possible to look around the corner of the near future and discern some of what lies ahead for this scrappy, visionary, and creative group of companies.

The base case for the segment's aggressive growth and expansion rests first on a broader definition, one that goes "Beyond Polar" and "Beyond Expedition," to include "Luxury Adventure," "Destination Exploration," "Cultural Discoveries," and "Immersive Experiences." Secondly, it rests on expanded geography. A myriad of nonpolar itineraries featuring Alaska, the Sea of Cortez, the Great Lakes, Central America, Galapagos, Australia's Kimberley, and more, including exotic rivers—Amazon, Mekong, and Irrawaddy. The farthest frontiers made more comfortably accessible and more familiar destinations revealed in new ways. The third ingredient is new markets and customers. China's affluent outbound travelers, baby boomers and millennials focused on the environment and experiences, and brand/loyalty partnerships such as Lindblad's World of Hyatt partnership.

Key to generating and serving increased demand is new ship construction and capacity expansion. The SeaTrade Cruise Order Book as of January 2020 reflected thirty-one new expedition builds for delivery through 2023. That's just one piece of the 150 new ships ordered for construction over the next six years.[17] Remarkable ship design, green technology, safety in remote regions, amenities that inspire the imagination and enable interaction with the natural world in amazing ways—submersibles, zodiacs, helicopters, underwater lounges, decktop glass-enclosed igloos, science labs, and extensive enrichment facilities and programs aboard ship. With increased visitor volume and interaction between guests and nature come concerns about over-tourism in fragile places, considering both ecological and cultural impacts. Operators are addressing these cooperatively through organizations such as IATTO and AECO and with communities visited.

Given these many growth-fueling factors, the sudden COVID-19 operational pause has been an unimaginable setback for even the

---

17   "Global Cruise Ship Orderbook Slims For 2021 and Beyond: Still Over 100 Ships," Cruise Industry News, February 9, 2021, www.cruiseindustrynews.com/cruise-news/24334-global-cruise-ship-orderbook-slims-for-2021-and-beyond.html.

best-positioned companies. There has been much focus on the circumstances and outlook of the mainstream cruise lines but little discussion yet about the unique challenges facing the specialized operators in this corner of the industry. The trajectory on which the business of expedition/adventure cruising was on will progress differently now due to new market realities and operating conditions. Companies will be challenged to adapt. There may be new opportunities as preference for small ships and uncrowded destinations increases, but also big challenges in staying the course financially and operationally.

Balancing assumptions about how long the nonoperating period will continue, how quickly demand will recover, and what the new business environment will entail is an imperfect science. Looking around the corner toward the near future, the next round of challenges and opportunities faced by the segment can be anticipated, along with strategies that may be employed to address them. In the movies, it may be possible to go "back to the future" but not in real life. New realities require new approaches.

Prior to COVID-19, there was already momentum toward expedition and adventure cruising. This trend may strengthen. However, there is a big difference between marketing and distributing into an expanding economy and marketing out of a hard stop, then rebuilding that previous momentum.

I see **six imperatives** facing the category:

Determining the Restart/Reboot Ramp—including timing, destinations, deployment, capacity, demand, regulatory compliance, costs, and the state of related travel infrastructure such as air service to remote destinations. A bright spot in 2020 could well be the US rivers and Great Lakes. The 2020 summer Arctic and Alaska seasons are largely lost, and the strength of the upcoming 2020/2021 Antarctica season is in question. The northern summer 2021 will most likely be the first opportunity for recovery, as will the 2021/2022 Antarctica season. The nonpolar destinations are likely to follow similar timing.

Access to Financial Resources—Companies must digest the combination of refunds, commissions, payables, debt service, vessel layup, and administrative costs during the pause, plus fund the reboot—bringing back staff and crew, vessel deployments and startup, marketing and sales, and much more customer-friendly deposit, change, and cancellation policies. It is a fundamentally different financial landscape. The largest publicly traded cruise groups are facing a collective monthly cash burn of nearly $1.5 billion, requiring new multibillion-dollar financings. Some of the smallest operators also face serious financial pressure. Even before these events, One Ocean Expeditions ceased operations due to financial difficulties. The prospect for acquisitions by larger cruise companies seem few since most have already branched into expedition.

Sorting Out New Builds—The impact that COVID-19 will have on shipyards, vessel delivery schedules, and order books is yet to be determined. There are already some announcements of delays in delivery dates. Scenic Group has plans for five additional sister ships to Scenic Eclipse. Perhaps all the anticipated thirty-one or more new ships will be delivered, but likely there will be changes to the schedule with some extended beyond 2023.

Marketing and Distribution—Tear up the old playbook. Companies must be prepared and organized for an agile, active approach to quickly discerning the new marketplace rules. Those who cautiously wait and hope for a recovery that lifts all boats will find themselves in a much smaller boat going nowhere fast. Energetic, agile, visionary, and innovative will win the day, flexing for uneven recovery among source markets and outperforming a field of competitors aggressively pursuing every potential customer. Speed to market will be critical as early movers will benefit the most. Radically differentiating—connecting emotionally, intellectually, and honestly while reaffirming customers' desires for life-changing experiences. Companies that embrace and demonstrably support their travel agent partners will be rewarded with enthusiastic and trusting professional advocates. Finally, companies should publish confident schedules through 2023 to demonstrate stability and their point of view about where the next best experiences will be found. For those who do this successfully, there is an opportunity to capture increased market share and to accelerate speed to recovery.

Sustainability—Health and Safety—COVID-19 makes clear in the sharpest terms the connection between the natural world and humans.

Thus this event deepens the appreciation for and understanding of the importance of sustainable lifestyles and practices. This will inform how and why more people will consume travel. Companies must address health/safety concerns directly, communicating both inspiration and reality. Customers should be trusted and respected with full transparency. Demonstrate sustainability—a commitment to the entire system/all stakeholders—guests, crew, communities, environment, nature, and business partners.

Protection of Pricing Integrity and Value Perception—Critical for a category with such fragile operating economics. There is little room for traditional cruise discounting practices to stimulate demand. These are extraordinary experiences. Guests make a considered calculation that I call the experience equation: $(EV) = X + Y + Z / (X)*(Y)$, where (EV) is experience value. This can absolutely be calculated based on variables including ship, itinerary, expedition team/enrichment program, price, season, et cetera. Guests, whether knowingly or not, make this calculation as part of a well-considered purchase. Personalization goes a long way toward protecting price integrity and value perception. Carefully crafting each piece of content, communication, and touchpoint is essential.

Finally, in light of the important innovations in sustainability, responsible tourism, purposeful and expansive guest experiences, and ship design, I expect this small but impactful segment will continue to influence the future directions of the larger cruise and travel industry, serving as a "bright beacon" in many respects. Onward!

• • • •

It's always nice to have clients follow your strategic recommendations and see them become real in the marketplace. The six imperatives proved hugely beneficial for all companies that adhered to them.

While my predictions came to pass and my advice based on prior experiences was spot-on, that's enough about the past. I prefer forecasting to hindcasting. While the past does not repeat, it rhymes. We take what we can from all that 2020 brought and look to the future with pragmatic optimism—and more than a little hope.

The six imperatives and protocols highlight different aspects of recovery that will keep you on track. Coming out of COVID-19 will require unprecedented patience and understanding of not only the economic implications but also the emotional impact all this has had on your customers, crews, and employees. Few people take time to understand what happened because they are consumed by what they are currently facing. Each protocol will help you harness a strategic advantage in that regard.

To that end, here is a graphic I've shared with cruise industry clients to help them readjust their focus from the present to the future: what I refer to as "Eyes on the Prize."

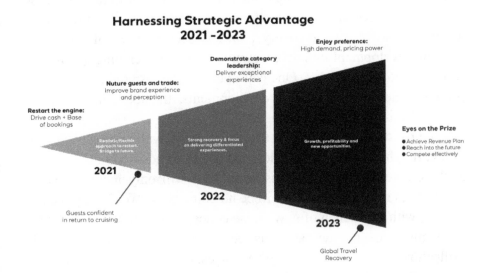

Harnessing Strategic Advantage 2021 -2023

Restart the engine: Drive cash + Base of bookings

Nuture guests and trade: improve brand experience and perception

Demonstrate category leadership: Deliver exceptional experiences

Enjoy preference: High demand, pricing power

Realistic/flexible approach to restart. Bridge to future.

Strong recovery & focus on delivering differentiated experiences.

Growth, profitability and new opportunities.

Eyes on the Prize
- Achieve Revenue Plan
- Reach into the future
- Compete effectively

2021

Guests confident in return to cruising

2022

2023

Global Travel Recovery

While we can look to the next decade and beyond, a clearer vision of what to expect comes as each year or quarter rolls in. The cruise industry necessitates a rolling three-year view or dashboard, given the logistics of ship building, deployment, itinerary and experience design, marketing, and global distribution. The future is a moving target, and you can adjust your aim as you get closer. Those in the industry who are able to adjust quickly and have flexible resources will be the ones to move forward. Companies with a positive, confident view and enough preparedness to ensure the right actions or pivots are taken will be the ones to lead the way out of COVID-19.

Because it will end. On the other side will be changes as challenging to those who are unprepared or underprepared. The virus may die out, but the disruption it brought never will. Disruption is three dimensional. There is the injury, the treatment, and the recovery. These can be called the concentric rings of disruption. Take Saudi Arabia as an example. They began transitioning their economy away from oil dependence, but this was accelerated by the impact of the COVID-19 pandemic. Not only did global travelers stay at home and lessen the economic contribution of international visitors, but the closures also affected trade at all levels. Saudi Arabia found themselves with insufficient domestic tourism and other similar domestic industries to replace their declining revenues. Part of their recovery plan has been a series of breathtaking new development initiatives, many aimed at developing a domestic cruise and tourism market. One can't help but be inspired by the vision behind some of the Red Sea developments, including the futuristic city of Neom.

The pandemic has dragged the cruise and travel industries into the future. In other words, the acceleration of key trends—technology, contactless, automation, safety, sustainability—will only increase. These are changes from which there will be no going back. We already see this coming with the launch of new cruise concepts right in the midst of the pandemic recovery, such as Atlas Ocean Voyages, Ritz Carlton Yacht Collection, Swan Hellenic, Virgin Voyages, and the recently announced developments of Cruise Saudi.

While the established cruise brands and markets were dealt a near death blow by the COVID disruption, they haven't stood still in their efforts to connect their fortunes to the future. MSC cruises has announced the first humanoid robotic bartender at sea, named Rob and featuring eight languages and a tech-forward set of skills. Royal Caribbean will continue to be the innovation leader among the major cruise groups, especially through their boundary-pushing Celebrity Edge series and Quantum Ultra Class ship platforms. Their Perfect Day at Coco Cay private island development will only inspire even more innovative cruise-land experience integration. Other major trends I expect to have an impact on the future direction of leisure and vacation travel include:

- Societal and demographic shifts
- Environmental changes
- Technological advancements
- Global economic trends
- Health concerns
- Tourism destination sustainability initiatives
- Marketplace competition

In the near and far future, successful travel companies will be those that adapt to outside forces, macro trends, and developments worldwide affecting their business. If my years of experience have taught me anything, it's that the cruise industry is uniquely positioned to shift when necessary. We already know how to remove the obsolete and reinvent ourselves, whether with ships or itineraries or incident responses or marketing campaigns.

The trends the cruise business will face can be viewed as potentially detrimental or beneficial. The industry wasn't able to fully prepare for COVID as we all would have preferred, but we can consider these predicted disruptions in advance and plan accordingly. The best way to navigate change is to view it as two corners—the near corner and the far corner.

The near corner is just out of our current visibility. We'll soon see it coming into view as the world turns and we with it. The near corner includes everything that's soon approaching. Since it's so closely connected to where we are, we can be pretty good at projecting with some accuracy what is coming—short of an unpredictable disruptive event, of course.

Then there's the far corner. The far corner is closer to an educated guess at what will happen five years from now and beyond. It's really a series of near corners revealing themselves one after another.

We can look into the future and see a lot of challenges that need to be overcome and opportunities to be realized. The future is curved like the horizon in that it disappears at a certain point. You can only see so far. Every situation is different. How far ahead do you think you can see? What do you assume lies beyond?

Know which direction you're going in, of course. If you are going to point as far as you can see, ask yourself if you are likely to continue in that direction. Can you see around the corner? Will you make a hard left or hard right? Is it possibly so different around the corner that you'll be zigging or zagging rather than making steady progress?

Planning ahead based on what you're able to anticipate lies in front of you prevents sudden directional changes that risk upsetting the passengers—family, employees, clients, et cetera—or worse, capsizing your business, career, or life.

Working through the six protocols is your best chance of making the next stage of life the best it can be. This framework will help you follow the trends and compare where you are to your competition. The protocols also give you an action plan for the most likely aspects of what is to come and some coping tools to handle the fog that blows in out of nowhere. It's never too late to make a course correction. Each of the six protocols gives you step-by-step info to practically prepare and encourages you to look into the future to see the positive things to come.

A few days after 9/11, I gave a speech to reassure fellow cruise industry leaders about the very near and very shrouded future. Those remarks ring true to this day.

> In the movies, it might be possible to go back to the future, but not in real life. The future will be different, and it will require new approaches and new solutions. I sincerely hope you will take the road less traveled in the months and years ahead. That you will forge new skills and develop new methods of delivering the cruise product to repeat and first-time cruisers.

I thought about saying "the sea less sailed," but having read the room, I could tell humor would not go over. So road, sea . . . whatever you want to call freedom from conformity, you'll need it in the months and years ahead.

The cruise business is and will forever be changed as a result of COVID-19—not so much by the long-term reaction of consumers who love cruise vacations as by regulators. To regulatory bodies, cruise ships represent giant science labs out in the real world. Few physical plants offer such a pristine and controlled environment in which millions of people of all ages and nations gather and remain together for a week or more at a time. This makes for an irresistible situation to observe, measure, test, and control. Airports, airplanes, hotels, theme parks, sports stadiums, and festivals are transient in nature and do not offer regulators and health officials the same opportunity to insert themselves.

But we can predict a new hypersensitivity and reaction to every public health matter as it pertains to cruising and cruise ships. Even health issues previously thought well handled, if not best handled, by the cruise business, such as the common norovirus, the flu virus, and food and water contamination, will gain renewed regulatory interest. Just as security measures such as TSA have exponentially expanded far beyond the event itself, so, too, will new health-related restrictions, oversight, and intervention. There's already a growing call for digital health passports backed by global heavyweights.[18] I suspect digital health passports will be a permanent fixture, like TSA and global entry. Add to that the likelihood of ubiquitous temperature screening, biometric scanning, and facial recognition. This will have an impact on the vacation experience itself, but even more so, on the cost of operating a cruise line. The price of a cruise will increase as a result. The growth rate of cruising could be affected. Customers and industry experts are already questioning how much fun they can actually have while enduring potentially invasive new health restrictions.[19] If they imagine they'll be socially distanced

18   Matthew Parsons, "NFL, Restaurateur Danny Meyer Back Digital Health Passports Through Investment in Clear," Skift, February 8, 2021, https://skift.com/2021/02/08/nfl-restaurateur-danny-meyer-back-digital-passports-through-investment-in-clear/.

19   Gene Sloan, "Why I'm Not Sure a 'Coronavirus-Safe' Cruise Sounds Like a Fun Time," The Points Guy, February 8, 2021, https://thepointsguy.com/news/cruise-ship-safety-plan-opinion/.

all day and night, surrounded by sanitization products and procedures, they'll be less likely to buy that ticket.

If you can accurately envision the opportunities and challenges of the near and further future, you are able to create actionable strategies and take action. Think for the near future and act now to be prepared for what's to come.

It's worth noting that my focus is the global cruise business. It is about far more than the ships. The business itself, and the people involved in the business at all levels, are what continuously drive my passion. So as we examine the future, we must keep our focus on the human impact and human potential.

I see an industry that is leading the way in diversity, safety, sustainability, and community responsibility. A diversity leader in the boardroom, in the offices, on board the ships, and in serving customers of all types.

Let's begin the journey together.

The Near Corner

Experience Normal Again: The Cruise Industry in 2020–2030

You can influence what comes around the corner through your actions today through diligence, quality work, innovation, teamwork, and clear-headed strategies.

I've thought about the future described in this way for quite some time. It's cocreation—you transform your thoughts into reality. Really, we all do it. Our actions, choices, and even our beliefs in the present moment affect what comes next. At every turn, you have a say in what happens. In the face of change, how you respond in the short term determines how you fare long term. To reach the far corners, you must first make it past the near ones. And what you experience *then* will be the culmination of the choices you make *now*.

That said, no human is yet capable of creating something out of absolutely nothing. We must start somewhere with something. Two of the building materials the cruise industry has to create in the near future are the reconfiguration of global cruise ship fleets and deployments and implementation of world-leading health protocols on board ships and ashore.

I suspect many companies coming out of the COVID disruption will consider joint venturing to share and reduce risk, speed things up, and gain capabilities and competence. Keep this in mind as COVID-19 recoveries happen across the board, regardless of what industry you're in. Big companies can do it, and so can you. Get creative and throw out the playbook. The small-company version of joint venture is a partnership. If you don't have the resources or connections, work with others. That goes whether you're a small adventure cruise line or a freelancer with an eight-to-five day job.

The cruise industry is not one monolithic entity made up of only the big oceangoing liners—consider contemporary, premium, luxury, river, expedition/adventure . . . Each segment will experience its own unique set of recovery challenges and path forward—driven by customers, geography, deployment, timing, and seasonality.

The new center of the cruise universe while in pause state will get smaller and more tightly compacted the longer the pause—as customers opt out, travel agents cease to operate, capacity is reduced, and new ship orders and deliveries are delayed. Thus, the expansion to come will be fueled by different dynamics than the industry went into the pause/contraction with—therefore it will expand to a different degree and in different directions. How powerful will that burst of energy be, in what directions, how fast, and for how long?

In North America, Australia, Asia, and Europe, there are large-scale efforts between and among cruise companies, governmental health agencies, immigration and customs authorities, airline companies, and infrastructure builders to coordinate a safe and sustainable restart of international travel generally and cruising specifically. The goalposts have kept moving as COVID-19 evolved into alternate strains and brought new outbreaks in areas we thought had recovered. Sometimes, it looked like the worst was over with, and we were ready to launch new initiatives. Then, all of a sudden, another ugly spike made everybody feel hesitant to move forward. It's unclear how the global pandemic will play out over the next couple of years. What is certain, however, are regulations. Contact tracing, mask wearing, social distancing, creating a bubble when going to shore, and other risk mitigation measures will be essential for cruise lines well into the 2020s.

Already, coronavirus vaccines are being deployed worldwide. The hope is that vaccinations will be the lasting solution to this whole pandemic. If the number of people who are willing to get the vaccine is high enough, offering a 100 percent–vaccinated cruise experience will be a home run. For example, I proposed to one client that we ride the wave of consumer sentiment and regulatory direction by getting out ahead of the market with a requirement that all guests and crew members be vaccinated on all future cruises, promoting the policy as "Experience Normal" to encourage guests to receive the vaccine and begin again enjoying their passion for travel.

This is an early mover advantage from a marketing standpoint. Yes, my client would lose the people who are uncomfortable with the vaccine or don't believe in vaccines, but the number of people who would be gained, who want a safe bubble to travel in, would make it more than worthwhile. That's something we can get a start on now, and a few clients already have. In early 2021, one of my clients took the bold step of mandating COVID-19 vaccination for all passengers, crew, and tour motor coach drivers. I pressed that they require as much from all guests and employees beginning with July 2021 sailings. They acted. And they've already begun to see improvement to top-line revenue.

It's obvious why I would advise this—and why the strategy will work. A strong attribute of the cruise industry has been unyielding commitment to health and safety. It's a unique environment, which is one of the pillars of cruising and is going to be of benefit in the coming years. We're already well adapted to the safety of our clients, and so we are able to quickly shift to new requirements. We're also better positioned than a lot of the tourism industry in that the ships can change destinations and demographics in order to rebuild stronger and keep up with the pace of innovation.

Yet until mass vaccination occurs, predictable operations will be difficult to achieve. The COVID equivalent of 9/11's TSA will be proof of vaccine and a negative test seventy-two hours before boarding a ship. There will be temperature detectors, much like there were metal detectors everywhere after 9/11. Cruise companies will be taking an even stronger offense and defense against all viruses because they are all too aware of the threats beyond COVID, including the seasonal flu and pervasive noroviruses.

Cruise marketing in the age of COVID means that customer-friendly, flexible-booking payment and cancellation policies are becoming the new competitive frontier. Due to constrained capacity during the restart and recovery period, pricing will not be the go-to tool of the cruise industry as in the past. Rather, addressing the concerns of consumers who have faced the frustration of delayed refunds or multiple cancellations and rebookings is the more pressing matter. Closely connected is the issue of travel adviser–supportive policies as relates to commissions, rebooking fees, and preserving pre-COVID tiered-commission levels. And, of course, clear communication about new protocols, such as the industry-leading "vaccination required" policy of some cruise lines.

Two additional long-lasting outcomes of COVID's impact on the cruise industry, beyond the financial, will be the accelerated reconfiguration of cruise fleets and the expansion of health-related regulatory measures. Carnival Corporation, for example, shed nineteen older, smaller, less efficient ships during the COVID pause. Royal Caribbean similarly removed vessels, including the sale of one of its smaller brands, Azamara, and its entire fleet. There are other examples across the industry. These moves, though inevitable, would have taken five-plus years to achieve; instead, they happened rapidly in a compressed time period. This means that the average ship's age went down, average ship size went up, and the earning power increased for each remaining ship in the fleet of the company to which it belongs. This will nicely match up with the many new builds coming out of the shipyards and under contract over the five years ahead. The positive effect of the new builds will be even more impactful on these reconfigured fleets. As the market recovers, the operating profit margins will soar. However, there will be a heavy load of debt and interest expenses that did not exist previously.

The second outcome will be overly burdensome regulatory oversight and involvement regarding health matters. The very strength of the cruise industry will be used against it. Regulators cannot help themselves. There is a bias against the cruise industry among many of them. COVID-19 will be an entree for strengthening the scope and scale of regulations that already exist, plus inventing new ones. International, national, regional, and local efforts will emerge and overlap, making for a very difficult operating situation and financial burden for cruise lines and intrusive measures for cruise travelers to accept.

In the coming years, health and safety will affect everything about cruising. Already, appreciation of and preference for safety are commonplace among travelers who aspire to return to cruising. An increasing share of such eager guests will expect to travel in smaller numbers and, most importantly, with like-minded guests when it comes to health, safety, and sustainability.

Thus, you can expect small ships and river cruises to lead the way in the cruise industry recovery. River cruises offer a more controlled setting. They are close to the shore and near medical resources, which can make guests more confident. Private groups and charters are options that allow for even more control.

Initially, the close-to-home and regional markets will literally drive demand as limited air service, cost, and desire to fly will dampen access to key port cities from further markets. Expect to see massive deployment of motor coaches and perhaps rail transportation services by cruise lines to extend their reach within regional markets.

The big cruise groups are not about to be left behind. Carnival Corporation, among others, has aggressively reduced the size of its fleet during the COVID pause, canceling scheduled trips and redeploying more of its fleet to close-to-home ports and markets in North America and Europe. The cruise industry has a lot of growth ahead of it, having penetrated a small share this far of the multitrillion-dollar global leisure travel industry. As that massive industry recovers and expands, so will the cruise business—perhaps at an even faster and more profitable rate and in new directions.

While companies are retiring or retrofitting old ships, they are also purchasing new ships that are designed with the niche traveler in mind. According to Cruise Industry News, thirty-two new small ships with seven thousand berths in total will enter the expedition adventure cruise market over a five-year period.[20] Expect a roller coaster ride as the high-flying segment absorbs astounding new capacity driven by new ships with fantastic new features enabling travelers to interact with nature in amazing ways, including submersibles, zodiacs, helicopters, underwater lounges, personalization tech, and extensive enrichment programs aboard and ashore.

Naval architect and designer Stefano Pastrovich predicted how technological innovation will align with the public's health and safety concerns to create a brand-new cruise experience:

> The companies will need to adopt a coordinated design solution of minor changes for their existing ships that include lightweight or soft compartmentalisation into protected areas, the conversion of buffets into restaurants, the creation of small closed-off public areas using Japanese-type walls—only made using fabric so they're easier to build and install, plus branded masks for all guests in addition to everything required for constant sanitising and cleaning. All this, together with the fall in contagion forecast for July and August, will reassure customers.[21]

---

20   "Expedition Orderbook Stands at 32 Ships, Over 7,000 Berths," Cruise Industry News, October 30, 2018, www.cruiseindustrynews.com/cruise-news/19862-expedition-orderbook-stands-at-32-ships-over-7-000-berths.html.

21   Teijo Niemelä, "Visionary Architect Stefano Pastrovich Offers Future Scenarios for the Cruise Business," Cruise Business Magazine, May 13, 2020, https://cruise-business.com/index.php/news-section/top-headlines-category/8675-visionary-architect-stefano-pastrovich-offers-future-scenarios-for-the-cruise-business.

These and other changes will create a halo effect for cruising. The industry will begin to highlight how a cruise ship, with its state-of-the-art HEPA filters and other safety measures, is one of the healthiest places on earth anywhere at any time.

Still, rebuilding ships into paragons of health will require more than standing room dividers, vaccines, and social distancing rules. We're talking about the redesign of what it means to take a cruise, beginning with the ships themselves and extending landside, including massive and sophisticated port facilities; private islands and ports; and multi-modal infrastructure involving air travel, ground transportation, and resort hotels. Of course, ships are floating cities, and no city is built in a day. They are designed and built over several-year periods. So here is what we can expect in the decades to come.

The Far Corner

Re: Cruise: The Cruise Industry in the 2030s and Beyond

The near future is just around the corner—always and relentlessly. The further future is similarly around a series of such corners. While we can't perfectly predict the future, we do know some basic principles about the character of that future. It will be strongly connected to and defined by the present. It will include ongoing change. The degree and scale of change are accelerating as a result of technology and communications. It will be shaped by a combination of circumstance and intentional actions that occur in the present.

We can both influence and prepare for the near and far future, to a degree. The transformation of the cruise industry and the accompanying opportunities and challenges are best understood by picking a point in the future that encompasses the announced new build capacity, envisioning what the industry looks like at that stage, and then looking back in time to the present to understand how we arrived at that future point and what lies beyond. There are presently 105 new ships under construction or announced on the horizon through 2026. That provides a tangible set of facts through which to envision the near-future influence of those new ship designs, the added capacity, and the new global customers they will attract to cruising.

There will be massive changes in shipbuilding, new materials and technologies, and more radical design in the ships when it comes to what's possible to retrofit old ships or build new ones. The not-so-distant future proceeding toward us is on the horizon today. China has already gotten itself into the cruise ship–building industry. Previously, only a few European shipyards were responsible. China is employing new shipbuilding materials and technologies to boot, making it faster and more efficient. I've seen them firsthand.

I served as advisor to a group that was pursuing a joint venture to develop the early domestic China cruise industry, an opportunity that came about due to disruption. Namely the 2008 establishment of China-Taiwan Cross Strait Relations, the first commercial connection between the two since 1949. Following the Great Recession, I traveled to China to work and negotiate with government and commercial entities on an early-stage cruise industry development project. In the course of that project, I gained valuable insight into the China travel market, distribution structure, and business and government culture. I came away from that deep-dive with a new appreciation for the disruptive potential of China as a player in the global economy. They play the long game, free of the short-term thinking that results from quarterly earnings targets. Decision-making takes a long time, but once decided, the ability to act quickly and at extraordinary scale is something one must see to appreciate. Chinese business and government leaders are disciplined and aligned in all of their actions. China's growing strength and global connections will influence and disrupt almost every aspect of our economy. A formidable competitor for future generations of United States business leaders and our workforce, be that the cruise, travel, and tourism industry or be that any other.

New ship designs are pushing the standards of safety ever higher, which is a good thing. The cruise ship of the future will be even more viable because it addresses the challenges and limitations of present-day cruising.

Companies that aren't ready to navigate through these changes will become obsolete quickly. Consider what happened when the boomers got on Facebook; Gen Y and Gen Z left. It's the same in cruising. How will this industry attract the next generations? The industry will have to redefine cruising itself. It will be harder to keep older vessels viable. What will become of them? Will companies succeed in repurposing ships?

We're already seeing ships two to three decades old sold for other uses or sent off to the scrapyards. Expect these occasional anecdotes to surge into a trend long term. It's going to be harder to keep these older vessels viable for as long as they've been able to keep them today. This could eventually affect cruise line financial balance sheets through accelerated depreciation models, shortening from thirty years to twenty. Fortunately, innovative ideas for what can be done with older vessels are appearing just in time. Some more radical suggestions have included low-income housing, centers for rehabilitation, or retirement villages because cruise ships are fully self-contained little cities.

Ultimately, cruising will be redefined in every way. Based on analysis of currently available information, there will be less friction and lower transaction costs. Eventually, blockchain technology will be put to use in the cruise industry, but not yet. There are layers of distribution that will first be redefined. Cruise companies will be able to support travel distributors directly with technology and AI tools. There will be many more individual travel advisers selling or distributing travel packages and cruises as a result, helping cruise lines penetrate more deeply into the next tiers/layers of market potential. There will be new pricing and payment models for cruise vacations, including subscriptions. Lock in your five-year cruising plan and spread the cost evenly over time via a convenient monthly subscription plan.

Hang on for an exciting ride and the emergence of great new industry developments over the five years ahead. While blockchain, AI, biometrics, digital health passports, and other technology won't transform the cruise industry into a sci-fi adventure overnight, the global future trends will require these innovative solutions to overcome upcoming issues.

One such issue will be the intersection of environmental sustainability and local favor. We will see preferred destinations shift to lesser-known alternatives. Local pushback has already begun, with communities like Venice, Italy, banning cruise ships. In Key West, Florida, the local residents passed a referendum in November 2020 that banned ships with more than thirteen hundred passengers from docking at their port.[22] Bar Harbor, Maine, began the process to enact similar measures. This is just the beginning of a trend in which cruise ships will not be welcome as often or in combination with others. There might be a one-ship rule in places where there used to be three, four, or five allowed at port at the same time.

In these highly coveted destinations, there comes a point at which the locals have had enough. For decades, cruise ships were their golden goose. Community leaders and small business owners loved all the money coming in from the tourists. COVID brought a reality check. Megaships and mega-crowds harmed their quality of life and brought potential risks in ways they had not had a pause to consider before. As more communities in tourist destinations make similar choices to Venice and Key West, where will the cruise ships go? As this shift happens, there will be more private port developments and private island developments by the cruise lines so they can maintain access to bucket-list regions around the world.

Together with the prerequisite technology, over-tourism will result in the cruise ship vacation concept going ashore. The ship is basically an island anyway. Why not turn an island into a ship, going beyond today's private island port calls? You'll be able to control the entirety of the customer experience. Currently, people get on giant ships to go to the Caribbean. At each port of call, guests who choose to do so leave the ship with a hurried few hours to sightsee, shop, visit colorful local bars

22   Barbara Smith, "Key West Residents Voted to Ban Large Cruise Ships from Docking—Whenever Cruises Resume," Business Insider, November 15, 2020, www.businessinsider.com/key-west-residents-vote-ban-large-cruise-ship-docking-2020-11.

and lovely beaches, snorkel, or enjoy whatever excursion thrills them. Then they're back on board before dinner for cocktails, entertainment, spa and gym visits, and fun at the casino. Note, these are all critical profit centers for today's modern large cruise ships, thus the need to get the guests back on the ship and depart from port for the most critical evening hours of spending and activity.

This routine will morph to more fully integrate the cruise and land experiences—perhaps going all the way to include some cruise-like vacations that occur entirely on fully developed private islands or new types of offshore floating but unmovable cruise platforms that guests reach via giant high-speed ferries. This would eliminate the need for port calls and the associated expense and impact. Many cruise guests in the Caribbean never leave the ship to go ashore; they are satisfied with all the facilities and amenities of the ship itself. A cruise island, real or in the form of a giant floating platform, would provide new alternatives for further developing the guest experience. More space, more options.

We're already seeing the early version of this concept. Big cruise lines own or have long-term leases on private islands in the Caribbean, the Dominican Republic, and the Bahamas to deliver this fantasy stop during the cruise. For example, I helped develop the Half-Moon Cay for Holland America in the Bahamas. It's a massive private island where passengers spend an entire day horseback riding, hiking, lying on the beach, or paragliding. I also was involved in the early stages of Icy Strait Point, a private port development in Alaska and the development of private railcars that extend the cruise experience into the heart of Alaska and chalet-style lodging at the doorstep of Denali National Park in Alaska.

As the traditional cruise transitions further to land-based extensions, you may expect the ocean cruise experience to also evolve in directions beyond imagination. Winged cruise ships are a new innovation on the horizon—wind- and solar-powered autonomously captained behemoths sailing untethered to traditional energy sources. Several countries in Asia have developed winged boats that glide on top of the water at high speeds.[23] Companies like Lockheed Martin are working on low-flying airships. Winged ships and other above-water cruise possibilities open up new destinations in shallower waters or hard-to-reach places: an evolution of the small-ship and yacht-cruising category.

Cruise concepts will continue to evolve in directions that enable guests to explore and redefine the far edges of experiential travel. Intellectual, purposeful, emotional, and physical interactions with the world. So what about a destination cruise to the moon? Why not? Space tourism is being developed now, so how long will it be until there is a CruiseX-type brand offering adventure cruises beyond earth? SpaceX and Virgin Galactic already have people lined up looking to spend a quarter of a million dollars to be launched just outside our atmosphere and float up there for a couple of minutes for a space experience. Why wouldn't a space cruise be viable as that industry expands? We already know how to do it.

If you're a science fiction fan and enjoy the dystopian view, cruise ships could evolve further as "smart cities" on the sea, enabling a tech-, health-, and information-privileged social class to live, work, and raise families remotely, free of the limitations and risks of land-based existence—crowding, crime, viruses, commutes. Take Santorini Island's history of early civilization as an example—their society became ultra-advanced relative to surrounding areas because they were able to advance unencumbered, free of invasion and disruption. Do I think this is likely? Probably not because it would take a lot of government changes to work. But is it possible? I can't discount it entirely. Perhaps the city of the future, Neom, under development on the shores of the Red Sea, is an early indicator.

It might seem out of the realm of possibility around a future corner, but be open to what is to come so you can steer in that direction if it fits your intent. You can also avoid being caught up in new trends that obviously don't fit, no matter how lucrative or profitable they seem. It's

---

23   Harry Valentine, "A Future for Winged Cruise Ships," The Maritime Executive, October 1, 2017, https://maritime-executive.com/editorials/a-future-for-winged-cruise-ships.

a navigational skill of finding a path through the unknown by relying on familiar skills and the preparation you've done with the six protocols.

Residential communities might be a bit more down-to-earth option for some companies looking into the future. Offering a lifestyle at sea for the wealthy might be an increasingly attractive option, whether it is in a tetrahedron-shaped super ship,[24] a floating hotel that drifts with ocean currents,[25] or something simpler. There is already a start in that direction. More likely, rather than short-term stays of a few days or weeks, ships configured as retirement communities would have a more stable, long-term clientele. The cost of a retirement community can be upward of $250 a day, 365 days a year; that's $91,000. There are people famous for taking hundreds of cruises. How big of a jump is it for seniors to enjoy the last of their healthy years living aboard, with the world's oceans and changing landscapes as their backyard?

This could be an answer to social issues as well. People who need a roof, education, meals, health, and rehab—it's all right there under one roof. This could be a place to use the retired cruise ships, subsidized by the government for affordable housing or rehabilitation. All the rooms and services are ready to go, and you don't have to build, fight over zoning, or have people complain, "Not in my backyard." Rehab on a ship might have some benefits for the patient's recovery as well. Even simply as a solution to homelessness, to get people off the street. There is a rising need for shelter in coastal cities worldwide. At the same time, the cruise industry is obsoleting their older vessels. One trend meets another . . .

For companies looking to stay closer to the realm of cruising that they're familiar with, technology and design advancements will offer a highly personalized experience for clients that is also easier for the

---

24   Tom Sweetman, "Tetrahedron Super Yacht: The Boat That Can Fly," CNN, March 14, 2016, www.cnn.com/2016/03/14/sport/gallery/tetrahedron-super-yacht/index.html.

25   "Mind-Blowing Floating Hotel Made to Drift with the Ocean Currents," Fox News, December 9, 2015, www.icyte.com/saved/www.foxnews.com/880336?key=d-ca1fc82818867daad2b4d8573f76546846759a3.

cruise operator to deliver. Tech-enabled options are popping up more and more frequently, so the cruise becomes a partnership between the customer and the cruise line, enabled by technology. That allows for a high degree of personalization and removes friction in order to increase revenue, profit, and guest satisfaction.

As an example, three years ago at the consumer electronics show (CES), Carnival Corporation announced Ocean Medallion, a vision of technology for personalized cruise experience.[26] They're running big ships with four or five thousand guests on board, all of them with a different ideal experience. One person wants to stay in the cabin the whole time and watch TV. Somebody else wants to be in the casino with a drink in hand. Another client goes to the gym every single day. There are all these different ways of having that experience: eating at different restaurants, taking part in different activities. Imagine if, as you approached the bar, no matter which bar, up came your picture, your name, and your preferred drink. As you approached the bar, the bartender called you by name and asked if you wanted your usual beverage of choice. That's an Ocean Medallion experience. It's wearable technology that allows the ship to see you as you travel. Big screens will pop up with personalized information to help you navigate your way through the ship. It also opens your door. It's total security. It's contactless in the new age of COVID and future viruses.

Royal Caribbean did it a little differently. Since everyone has their own smart device, they're building an app that offers passengers a similar personalized experience. Other companies are considering something like the equivalent of Alexa in each cabin. In this way, technology makes the cruise a smoother process as it can help out and share the workload. A cruise ship can only hold so many crew members to serve so many customers. That means there's a maximum number of waiters at each bar. In peak hours, right before or after a show or during the dinner hours, those bars can be under great pressure.

---

26   Consumer Technology Association, n.d., www.ces.tech/Exhibitors/Success-Stories/OceanMedallion.aspx.

What if, instead of waiting to order your drink, the menu pops up in front of you, and you can order as soon as you're ready. Then the waiter can focus on delivering drinks rather than trying to make the rounds taking orders. It's a tiny change that will make a big change in smoothing out operations. That's the future of tech. There's this unique partnership between customer, crew members, the cruise line, and technology that equals a better experience for all.

Themed cruises and special interest cruises open up a world of opportunity, with so many options from sports, wine, or music to any other interest or trend.[27] Technology will also allow companies to offer unique experiences to new customers for targeted adventures. Augmented reality will be adopted broadly and virtual reality in specific applications. Think about the phenomenon of the gaming industry. People pay a ton of money to watch gamers. It's all virtual reality, and a gaming company could take over a cruise ship and have that be a place that their champions and their audience come to watch these multimillion-dollar gaming events. In this way, a cruise ship could become a platform for different types of experiences. Cruise ships could even become tax-advantaged havens for sports events or video game competitions on the high seas in international waters.

Of course, all this requires a faster internet with better signals. Low-orbit satellite networks can do just that, accelerating digital connectivity availability at sea. This solves the problem of high-speed internet being unavailable in remote international waters. Cruise ships will now be able to have high-speed internet and all the advantages that come with it. The twenty-four-seven connectivity, the speed of connectivity, and the volume of data that can travel through that connectivity are only going to keep getting better and better and better. That opens even more possibilities for a cruise ship and its passengers to fully leverage the digital resources that exist on land while at sea.

Other future considerations move beyond technology and design into geopolitical areas.

---

27   Brian Johnston, "The Future of Cruising: What You Can Expect to See in the Next Decade," Traveller, September 30, 2017, www.traveller.com.au/essay-the-future-of-cruising-gyofwc.

I predict cruise ships will return to Cuba right around the corner with the US administration change. Cruises were banned from traveling to Cuba by the Trump administration. I could see that changing back again.

I also foresee an increase in consolidation. Instead of cruise companies buying other cruise lines, I see other companies buying cruise lines because they're consumer platforms. Disney is already an example. Entertainment and hospitality brands will bring new elements to the industry. Disney Cruises fuse entertainment and cruising. Disney, of course, brings all its characters on board and a whole experience that cruising could never do on its own. What else might be possible with other combinations of big players out there in the hospitality, entertainment, gaming, and media business landscape?

Overall, hotel hospitality brands will delve further into the cruise industry, and we'll start to see a blurring of the lines as tastes change and new demographics take up cruising. Eventually, China and India will be the biggest markets in the world for cruising. China's middle class is bigger than the entire US population. I think certainly Eastern Europe and Russia will see an increase as well.

These new growth areas will need to be balanced with an increased call for sustainability.

Cruise lines have really great programs in place to mitigate pollution and environmental concerns. I think that's just going to continue to be a driver of the industry with more self-regulation and government-imposed regulations. Some brands are building LNG-powered ships for a cleaner-burning fuel.[28] Fuel cells are coming as well, operating without harmful emissions, producing only water vapor. Ships are also being built with autonomous systems that can streamline navigation and incorporate green technology. Other eco-conscious cruise lines have adopted a "no disposable plastic" rule, so there are no straws or other throwaway amenities. Most ships today have whole wastewater plants so that the water that's going off the ship into the ocean is cleaner than the ocean water itself. It's an amazing part of the industry.

---

28   Jeff Desjardins, "The Future of Shipping Is Green and Autonomous," Visual Capitalist, December 20, 2017, www.visualcapitalist.com/future-shipping-green-autonomous/.

In the future, the pressure to do more from a sustainability perspective will steadily continue. Regulations are becoming more serious to counteract poor environmental choices. The cruise industry is aware that their actions affect local ecosystems. I lived in the Seattle area for years, and just north of us, the city of Victoria, British Columbia, for decades did a really poor job of managing wastewater coming out into the ocean. Raw sewage was dumped into the waters and carried by the currents that run down the coastline. Those currents brought that stuff right into Puget Sound on the doorstep of Seattle, having a negative impact on the local water quality. Finally, in 2021, Victoria installed a $500 million wastewater plant to begin curbing these practices. The cruise industry, on the other hand, is a commercial enterprise. So it's much easier to regulate, which is why cruise lines have had sophisticated wastewater plants, solid waste management and recycling, and stack emissions scrubbers for decades and, recently, more earth-and ocean-friendly fuel sources, like LNG and, eventually, hydrogen. I believe the cruise industry will continue to lead the way among all industries when it comes to implementing new practices and policies.

The future disrupts. Time disrupts. Odds are you will live longer. Odds are the cost of everything will keep going up, especially health care. Odds are your income and any assets you have will be taxed at ever-higher rates. There will be no traditional retirement for anybody other than the comfortably wealthy and those who were financially astute throughout their careers. Don't stop producing, contributing, and mentoring until you have to. This is important for yourself, your long-term security, and the community at large. Live and lead by example. To do that, you must become adept at successfully dealing with disruptions of all types.

Act now. Follow the near corner into the future. Expand your horizons. And take steps now toward where you want to be in the long term. Make your own footprints in the future.

That's what winners do.

Onward!

David Giersdorf
Bend, Oregon
March, 2021

5 Ways to Get David's Help Directly

Want free updates from the author? Join David A. Giersdorf's email list for up-to-date, need-to-know cruise, travel, and tourism industry news. You'll also be notified about new products such as the upcoming *Hard Ships* masterclass. Simply subscribe at www.DavidGiersdorf.com.

Ready to align your team with a proven process to outlast disruption? Buy *Hard Ships* for your organization, leadership team, C-suite, board, team, or family. Email Contact@DavidGiersdorf.com for more information.

Need a guest speaker to inspire your team? Request David A. Giersdorf to speak at your event, deliver a workshop, or address your team remotely. Email Contact@DavidGiersdorf.com for more info.

Want expert advice? Get David A. Giersdorf's advisory services for your C-suite or board. Expertise includes growth, performance, product development, acquisitions, marketing, sales, distribution, and emerging technologies.

David is also available to implement his recommendations with his hand-picked team to create your bespoke solution. Email Contact@ DavidGiersdorf.com for more.

Need more revenue? Access the Global Voyages Group proprietary marketing database for cruise, travel, and tourism marketers. Contact David@GlobalVoyagesGroup.com.

Acknowledgements

The voyage that carried me to authoring this book included many fellow travelers, who were beacons that shed light on my uncharted course.

To my wife, Peggy—thank you for riding out the storms with me.

To my kids, Nicholas and Caitlin—thank you for helping to keep the ship upright.

To my sister, Debbie—thank you for being there when it was just the two of us facing the world.

To my father Robert and stepmother Lori—thank you for showing the way.

To my many friends and colleagues through the decades and adventures—thank you for your no-holds-barred guidance and unconditional support.

And to the men and women of the global cruise industry, especially the ones aboard the ships who make it all work—thank you for inspiring me everyday.

I owe an unpayable debt of gratitude to you all. Thank you.

About the Author

David A. Giersdorf is an innovative entrepreneur with extensive C-suite experience in the cruise, travel, and tourism industry, including senior executive leadership positions at Holland America Line, Windstar Cruises, Paul Gauguin Cruises, American West Steamboat Company, and Exploration Cruise Lines.

David is Founder of Global Voyages Group, a CEO-level advisory engagements firm addressing growth, performance, product development, acquisitions, marketing, sales, distribution, and emerging technologies. He is also an advisor and limited partner of Seven Peaks Ventures. Previously, he was Managing Director and CEO of CF2GS, an award-winning marketing services firm acquired by True North Communications.

David is a former Chairman of Cruise Lines International Association (CLIA) and numerous other industry and civic organizations. Giersdorf attended the University of Washington and completed a Northwestern University Kellogg School of Management Program in Entrepreneurship.

David is also the author of *Hard Ships: Navigating Your Company, Career, and Life through the Fog of Disruption*, which details his four decades of experience navigating brutal disruptions to achieve innovation and growth.

David greatly enjoys helping companies and their teams envision the opportunities and challenges of the near and further future, innovate continuously, and create sustainable value for all stakeholders. Companies, clients, and close friends know David for disrupting disruption. When disruption is upon you, there is what happens around you, how it affects you, and what you are going to do about it. Do the opposite of nothing, David advises. Learn more about David, *Hard Ships*, and his advisory work at www.DavidGiersdorf.com.